*Executions and the British Experience
from the 17th to the 20th Century:
A Collection of Essays*

EXECUTIONS AND THE BRITISH EXPERIENCE FROM THE 17TH TO THE 20TH CENTURY: A COLLECTION OF ESSAYS

edited by William B. Thesing

McFarland & Company, Inc., Publishers
Jefferson, North Carolina, and London

British Library Cataloguing-in-Publication data are available

Library of Congress Cataloguing-in-Publication Data

Executions and the British experience from the 17th to the 20th
  century : a collection of essays / edited by William B. Thesing.
      p. cm.
    Includes bibliographical references (p. 165) and index.
    ISBN 0-89950-452-3 (lib. bdg. : 50# alk. paper) ∞
    1. Capital punishment—Great Britain—History.   2. Executions and
  executioners—Great Britain—History.   3. Capital punishment in
  literature.   4. Executions and executioners in literature.
  I. Thesing, William B.
  HV8599.G8E94   1990
  365.6'6'0941—dc20   90-6531
                                                                          CIP

Manufactured in the United States of America

McFarland & Company, Inc., Publishers
  Box 611, Jefferson, North Carolina 28640

For Jane and Amy

Contents

Contents

"—and the lark has not yet finished his flight:
you can see and hear him yonder in the fringe of a white May cloud."
— Alexander Smith
"A Lark's Flight" (1863)
(an essay upon an execution)

Introduction

In March 1987, a special session entitled "Executions and the British Experience" was held at the annual meeting of the Philological Association of the Carolinas held at the University of North Carolina–Greensboro. The original members of the panel – all of whose papers are included here – were Gayle R. Swanson, Steven Lynn, Barry Faulk, and William Thesing. After the papers were read, there was a lively and enthusiastic discussion period. In fact, there was not time to deal with all of the questions from the audience. Clearly a topic of intense and important substance had been discovered; many further questions and issues needed to be investigated. Afterwards some conferees suggested that the project should be expanded into a permanent collection of essays. Research has been spurred by curiosity and interest in the topic; the debate can now continue between the hard covers of this volume. It should be added that all of the essays are original and written expressly for this collection; however, because Steven Lynn's essay won the Joiner Prize for outstanding conference essay, it was published in the organization's journal, *Postscripts*, in 1988. The editor, Debra Boyd, and the association have generously granted permission for the essay to appear here as well.

In a recent book entitled *Capital Punishment and the American Agenda* Franklin E. Zimring and Gordon Hawkins argue that with "1,700 prisoners on death row throughout the country and an accelerating execution rate, it is more urgent than ever before for America to make decisions on the future of the death penalty." Many American sociologists have written on the issue of the ultimate punishment. Charles E. Silberman in his noted study, *Criminal Violence, Criminal*

Justice, offers many insights concerning the questions of crime and punishment. He writes: "On the contrary, recent research on deterrence suggests that increasing the certainty of punishment has considerably more impact on crime than does increasing its severity." Further, he writes: "I am not proposing that the debate over the death penalty be stilled; I suggest only that we recognize that the case for and against it is based on moral and political, rather than empirical, considerations.... justice can be purchased at too high a price."

The controversy over the death penalty in Great Britain ended with its total abolition in 1983. As Leon Shaskolsky Sheleff explains in his new comprehensive study, *Ultimate Penalties: Capital Punishment, Life Imprisonment, Physical Torture*, abolition did not have universal support: "In Britain ... there has always been strong support for capital punishment, both from the highest echelons of government and from expressed public opinion. Yet, in 1983, comprehensive and controversial debate in Parliament led to an historic decision for total abolition. This was the culmination of a struggle against the death penalty that had begun over a hundred years earlier, [and] had aroused intense passions on both sides of the debate." About two years later (January 21, 1985) an article appeared in the *New York Times* entitled "Texas Execution Is Third in the Nation in a Week." It is estimated that right now there are 2,100 inmates on death row in the United States. Clearly, in over a dozen states in America the issue is a life-and-death matter. Beyond the prisoners' fates, it is vital that citizens of a modern Western democratic society understand the moral, legal, and political questions raised by the imposition of capital punishment. Sheleff explains why the capital punishment debate is currently one of society's *major* moral issues: "Few issues in the realm of penal law theory and penological practice have aroused as much controversial debate as that of capital punishment. The extremity of the act, the irrevocability of its consequences, the power of its impact, have given it both a substantive and a symbolic quality which distinguishes it from any other sanction used by society to punish its transgressors.... At stake is not merely what is to be done with transgressors, but how society perceives itself and its commitment to human rights and social decency."

Are there lessons for American citizens in examining the British experience with executions over four centuries? The contributors to this collection obviously believe that there are and they find the most fascinating responses to the issue in works written by poets, novelists, prose writers, and philosophers. These essays examine the wide-ranging literary and philosophical response to executions in Great Britain between 1649 and 1936. In doing so, this collection of essays offers a wider perspective on the American debate over capital punishment by examining the psychological, philosophical, literary, and historical responses to executions in Great Britain over a time span that covers parts of the 17th, 18th, 19th, and 20th centuries. The essays offer some historical and cultural perspective on the current debate concerning capital punishment; they draw on the multifaceted British experience with this important social issue in order to provide a background against which to measure some of the current—and often very narrowly focused—debates by American sociologists and politicians.

An explanation of the dates that serve as the parameters for this collection of essays is necessary. January 30, 1649, is the date that Charles I, king of England, was beheaded. For over a century after his execution, he became an English national symbol—a touchstone of opposing political and moral values. He was viewed as either a holy martyr or a ruthless tyrant. At the other end of the story stands a commoner: Michael Barrett, a 27-year-old Irish stevedore and convicted Fenian terrorist, who was the last person to be executed publicly in England, on May 26, 1868. However, several essays speculate on the echoes and reverberations of the execution experience through the 20th century, until total abolition was passed by Parliament in 1983.

Donald T. Siebert's essay focuses on the topic of royalty and executions, with specific reference to Charles I and the legends that his death fostered. His essay is based on research that he conducted with a University of South Carolina Research and Productive Scholarship grant in the British Museum and the Bodleian Library, Oxford. Steven Lynn's research began while he was on a Folger Fellowship studying Locke and language theories with Hans Aarsleff. His essay studies Locke's influence on Cesare Beccaria, whose works had widespread intellectual appeal in both the 18th and 19th centuries. He examines the psychological model on which Beccaria based his ideas about capital punishment. Gayle R. Swanson's essay focuses on Henry Fielding as a writer and a London magistrate. The great benefit that the gallows could provide to the citizens of England lay, in Fielding's opinion, in its singular power to deter crime. In his writings he sought to educate the general public about social responsibility and the law. John J. Burke, Jr., in his essay focuses on Samuel Johnson's role in the case of the Reverend Dr. William Dodd, who was executed on June 27, 1777. He also examines how that role was presented in the rival biographies by Hawkins and Boswell. These two biographies were published shortly after Johnson's death in 1784 and are themselves examples of the range of attitudes toward capital punishment in late 18th-century England.

In his essay Barry Faulk argues that the political shift from the 18th-century "mob" to the 19th-century "crowd" brought about a corresponding shift in the literary representation of the masses. Nineteenth-century representations of the crowd by such writers as Dickens and Thackeray were reliant on certain key rhetorical devices, devices not without political implications. F. S. Schwarzbach characterizes a pattern of ambivalence about capital punishment in Charles Dickens's essays and novels that treat the subject. His famous letters to the *Daily News* in 1846 argue that public executions degrade the populace and only encourage violent crime. His objection to public hanging notwithstanding, throughout his fiction, early and late, he presents scenes in which villains are dispatched in violent ways without a hint of authorial disapproval. In her essay Beth Kalikoff uses a feminist and interdisciplinary approach; she examines some Victorian street literature — specifically, "gallows literature" — and demonstrates that the execution of female killers had quite a different impact on viewers than the execution of male murderers did. She relates these patterns to hangings depicted in the works of Thomas Hardy. William B. Thesing's essay examines the response by poets in the high literary tradition to hangings. He argues that the writings of William Wordsworth, Coventry Patmore, and A. E. Housman clearly reflect a change in the conception of the nature and function of the poet over the century. Michael Jasper's essay links violent crowd reactions to similar ritualized events held in Roman amphitheaters; he also links the Victorians' obsession with purchasing execution relics with medieval spiritual attitudes. The final essay in the volume allows David D. Cooper, a noted authority and historian, to reexamine a topic that he explored in a book published in 1974. He offers some reflections on and additions to his previous study on the lessons to be learned from the public execution controversy. The links that he makes between Victorian Fenian activities and modern terrorist activities practiced by the IRA in Northern Ireland and sometimes in England again demonstrate the intricate connections of history. Crime and punishment is a topic that continues to perplex modern societies.

– William B. Thesing
Columbia, South Carolina

The Aesthetic Execution
of Charles I: Clarendon to Hume

DONALD T. SIEBERT

1

When describing the execution of "the ROYAL MARTYR King Charles the First," Laurence Echard overcharges his narrative with drama and special effects to mark that event as one of the most reverberating in world history. Only a half century after the deed the beheading of Charles has already assumed the form and language of mythology. All nature, all humankind react in sympathy. The "last Scene of this Tragedy" happened on "a very cold dark Day"—"a Day melancholy & dismal beyond any that *England* had ever yet beheld." Charles looked "round upon the vast Throngs of People, who with bleeding Hearts and weeping Eyes press'd to behold this dismal Spectacle." After the dreadful martyrdom, there seems no limit to Echard's hyperbole: "None of the kings of *England* ever left the World with more open Marks of Sorrow and Affection. The venerable Archbishop *Usher*, from a Window, swooned at the sight of the fatal Blow, as at a Prodigy too great for Heaven to permit, or the Earth to behold: And as the Rumour of his Death spread throughout the Kingdom, Women miscarry'd, many of both Sexes fell into Palpitations, Swoonings and Melancholy, and some, with sudden Consternations, expired."[1] Perhaps no execution scene except the Crucifixion itself has ever inspired such attention in art, particularly literature. That the resulting art was not always wholly successful is apparent, as we see from Echard's bombast, but the scene of Charles's execution might nonetheless be termed highly mythopoeic.[2]

The *ars moriendi* tradition was strong in the 17th and 18th centuries.

How a person died was important; it was expected that good people would die well, and that the good *and* great would die greatly. And what conditions offer more challenges, and hence opportunities, for greatness, than suffering an execution? Even the ephemeral, the supposedly "inartistic," writing of the time reveled in descriptions of these events, in particular focusing on the behavior and last words of the condemned. Throngs were witness to the executions of poor wretches at Tyburn, but many more devoured written descriptions of how the felons died, and what they said. There, at the doorstep of eternity, the condemned could be seen as destined for either salvation or damnation.[3]

Thus one *read* the execution scene. It was a text to be interpreted — and almost invariably moralized. How does Echard read the execution of the regicides, as they later received what was for him the most condign punishment? In stark contrast to Charles's glorious martyrdom, their exit is a revolting extermination. (We must remind ourselves, however, that Echard's intended audience was more inured to brutal executions, and certainly readier to accept them as just and fitting, than a modern reader would be.)

> *Harrison* ... was first hang'd with his Face towards the *Banquetting-House* [where Charles had been beheaded], and then, being cut down alive, his Body was quarter'd and plac'd upon the City Gates, and his Head upon *Westminster-Hall* [where Charles had been condemned].... To aggravate the Severity of these Executions,... when *Cooke* was drawn upon his Sledge [which carried him to his execution], the Head of *Harrison*, with his Face uncover'd [three days after his execution, one notes], was plac'd before him to the great Detestation of the People.... When his Body was cut down and quarter'd, the Executioner, rubbing his bloody Hands together, came to *Peters*, then going to suffer, and ask'd him *How he lik'd that Work?* (779)

Echard later relates in gloating detail how most of these pitiful scoundrels were besotted with strong drink for the occasion. He is scandalized that some of Carew's partisans would have described his fuddled countenance as "*shining with great Glory.* As to *Hugh Peters*, he had taken so large a Potion, that he for some time behaved himself like an Ideot, and was stupidly drunk" (780).[4]

Thus not every execution in the historical literature of this age might be termed "aesthetic," unless we use the term with some license. Much as in classical theories of tragedy, only great people are privileged to suffer beautiful deaths, the kind immortalized by the muse Clio. The deaths, indeed the executions, of ordinary people do not merit that kind of treatment. It is not that commoners cannot die well, but they never come onto center stage. Quite unlike Echard, David Hume feels no disposition to exult in the deaths of the regicides. He may have been just as sympathetic to Charles and just as hostile to the king's enemies, but when ready to tell of their executions in his *History of England*, he asks his readers to pity them and implies at least—to our surprise after reading Echard—that they died well: "No saint or confessor ever went to martyrdom with more assured confidence of heaven than was expressed by those criminals, even when the terrors of immediate death, joined to many indignities, were set before them."[5] That is all he will say. Hume will spend no time describing that kind of scene. "Terrors" and "indignities" inflicted on "criminals" are not the stuff of great art— nor the subject of exultation for a man of feeling, as Hume the writer might justly be called.[6] As we shall see later, among the writers of British history in the 17th and 18th centuries, Hume stands out as the most theoretically conscious of art, and never in the six volumes of his *History of England* does Hume feature any execution except that of a great figure.

<h2 style="text-align:center">2</h2>

Without question the preeminent execution available for meaningful treatment by these historians was that of Charles I. Still, not any transcription of an event succeeds in being art, or in terms of contemporary theory, performs equally well in narrativizing past events. Unlike full-fledged history, the chronicle does not select and arrange its details artfully, nor does it completely narrativize. The chronicle lacks purposeful shaping, moral design—indeed, a beginning, a middle, and an end: narration simply continues until it stops.[7] That is not to say that a chronicle is completely deficient in meaning or effectiveness, but it lacks many of the features that we normally think of as belletristic. Let us examine two such accounts.

John Rushworth's *Historical Collections* (1659–1701) and Bulstrode Whitelock's *Memorials* (1682) are similar, contemporary chronicles of the Civil Wars that serve as quasi-official and reputedly impartial versions of the king's beheading; both are primary sources for the 18th-century historians of the event.[8] In these accounts everything included comes exactly when it happened or was noticed. As he faithfully records every word of the king's last speech, Whitelock also interrupts it right at the moment when the king interrupts himself: "For the king, indeed I will not—then turning to a gentleman that touched the axe he said,—Hurt not the axe that may hurt me. For the king, the laws of this land...." (2: 514). In Rushworth the king comes upon the scaffold, notices the great crowd of people, walks around the scaffold and looks "earnestly" at the block, asks if it could not be higher, then speaks to those present on the scaffold (7: 1428). Nothing is made of his understandable concern and the fortitude he displays, and there is no explanation of why he does not address the many other spectators: actually, they were kept too far away, and so the king did not try.

To be sure, there are individual sentences with memorable graphic power: "This Day his Majesty was brought from St. *James*'s, about 10 in the Morning, walking on foot through the Park, with a Regiment of Foot for his Guard, with Colours flying, Drums beating, his private Guard of Partizans, with some of his Gentlemen before, and some behind, bear-headed [sic]" (Rushworth, 7: 1428). Here the motley, confused assortment of details captures quite well the excitement and anticipation of the great scene: even the tautological "walking on foot" seems appropriate to a sort of writing to the moment that will never be improved, or falsified, by art. Overall these accounts simply tell what could be observed, *whenever observed*, from the trivial to the momentous, from the touching to the bizarre. The climax itself has only the power of quick narration in a lean style: "After which the King stooping down, laid his Neck upon the Block; and after a little pause, stretching forth his hands, the Executioner at one blow severed his Head from his Body. Then his Body was put in a Coffin" (Rushworth, 7: 1430). In the deadpan manner of the stereotypical police investigator, we get just the facts.[9]

3

Of those historical narratives to which we might be willing to ascribe aesthetic features, there are two types, the intimate and the distant. In the first we are there on the scaffold, as we are in the chronicle, but we are not so insulated from emotional response by the chronicle's haphazard factuality and objective reporting. Echard represents this type, but his contemporary White Kennet is a more effective practitioner. Although the two historians' accounts are quite similar in many respects, Kennet is less inclined toward fustian, less disposed to moralize and wail "alas," more skillful in arranging details for cumulative emotional power. In general he is more novelistic; though not writing in the first person, he reminds one of Defoe: he displays a similar unstudied, faltering narration that conveys immediacy and sincerity, and his accretion of detail can be overwhelming.

We join the king on the night before his execution, sleeping four hours, waking early and calling to his valet Herbert, who has slept fitfully on a pallet beside the king, to fetch his best clothes, for today is his "second Marriage-Day" and before night he hopes "to be espoused to [his] blessed Jesus."[10] He also must dress warmly so as not to shake from the cold and give the impression he is afraid. When Bishop Juxon later reads from Matthew 27 on the Passion of Christ, the king is pleased with the choice and even more so when he learns that this passage *happens to be* the lesson for the day in the liturgy: "the King . . . thought it a providential Preparation for his Death" (3: 186). In the succeeding narration of the events leading up to the scaffold, Kennet's is much like other accounts, including the chroniclers'. In transcribing the king's final speech, he even records the interruption regarding the gentleman who touches the ax. As in many other versions, Charles asks Colonel Hacker, officer-in-charge, that they not put him to pain (3: 186–87). In these passages Kennet is preferable to other historians only in writing more gracefully. And occasionally one might prefer Echard, who explains why the king has a portion of bread and claret after communion: namely, to ensure that he would not tremble in the cold weather outside and thus look afraid.

Kennet's decided superiority is evident in the very last scene, however. Here is the passage that follows Charles's quasi-liturgical words with the bishop about exchanging a temporal crown for an eternal one. Formal speeches and obligatory professions of faith are now over:

> Then the King ask'd the Executioner, *Is my Hair well?* And taking off his Cloak and George [Order of St. George], he deliver'd his George to the Bishop, saying, *Remember*. Then putting off his Doublet, and being in his Wastecoat, he put on his Cloak again, and looking upon the Block, said to the Executioner, *You must set it fast*. The Executioner saying, it was fast; the King said, *It might have been a little higher*. Being told by him it could be now no higher, the King said, *When I put out my Hands, then.* – And saying a few words to himself as he stood, with Hands and Eyes lift up, immediately stooping down, he laid his Neck upon the Block, and the Executioner again putting his Hair under his Cap, his Majesty thinking he had been going to strike, bad him *Stay for the Sign;* to which the Executioner said, "Yes I will and it please your Majesty." So after a short pause, his Majesty stretching forth his Hands, the Executioner (who was all the while in a Mask) at one Blow severed his Head from his Body, which being held up and shewed to the astonish'd People, was with his Body put into a Coffin covered with black Velvet, and carried into his Lodging-Chamber in *Whitehall.* (3: 187)

One would have to read many other accounts to appreciate this one fully. In many, these details are scattered elsewhere – indeed even as early as before the final speech – and the terrible beheading is gotten over with rather quickly. In contrast an unbearable suspense gradually builds in Kennet's much lengthier version of what passed between final formalities and the execution itself. One senses the king's anxiety that there be no unseemliness and pain, and perhaps an unconscious attempt to delay the fatal moment. He minds himself with all the little details, taking off and then putting on his cloak again. Is his hair out of the way, can't the block be higher – as it was, he had to lie prostrate rather than kneel – is the block fast enough, does the executioner understand the sign? Reinforcing the impression of anxiety, Kennet emphasizes the king's last-minute panic that adjusting his hair again means that the executioner is about to strike before the sign.

And the climactic sentence itself deserves praise. Echard writes in passive tense, "his Head was at one Blow sever'd from his Body" (661) – obscuring the image of headsman and ax, the very terrifying force of the blow, the fact indeed that at this moment the state, embodied by its executioner, has chopped off its sovereign's head. Kennet's sentence is more dramatic and meaningful. He employs the same syntax as Rushworth: subject, adverbial phrase, verb, object. From the executioner's raised arms, the ax descends and then comes the single reverberating blow, and then the head falls off. It is a clear line of force whose origin and object are dreadfully clear. But to Rushworth's sentence Kennet inserts "(who was all the while in a Mask)" between "executioner" and "blow." The phrase suspends the ax for a second and shocks the reader with a sudden image suggesting the macabre, sinister dimension of the act. Most writers make careful note of the two heavily disguised executioners, usually at the beginning when the king steps onto the scaffold; Kennet concentrates the detail into one masked executioner, and he unveils it only at the last.

Kennet thus orchestrates his details to maximize the emotional impact. Echard, for example, in his opening description of the black-draped scaffold, mentions that beside the block and ax were "Hooks and Staples to drag [the king] to Execution, should he make any sort of Resistance" (660). This initial image is quite chilling and effectively suggests the king's courage. Echard's version may be the better here. Still, it is interesting that Kennet again saves the detail until after the execution is over, devoting a paragraph to it. Apparently he wants to prolong the reader's feeling of outrage and horror. "It must be dreadfully remember'd," he says, "that the cruel Powers did suspect, that the King would not submit his Head to the Block; and therefore to bring him down by Violence to it, they had prepared Hooks and Staples (made by a Smith in *Aldgate*) to hawl him as a Victim to the Slaughter" (3: 187). Intensifying the brutality suggested by the hooks and staples, Kennet adds the starkly violent words "hawl," "Victim," and "Slaughter." The phrase "(made by a Smith in *Aldgate*)" is a touch reminiscent of Defoe—a phrase both awkward and yet peculiarly successful. One might argue, of course, that it distracts from the starkness of the image. On the other hand, it functions in terms of circumstantial realism to authenticate the horror—this is no fairy tale made up to frighten children—and likewise provides a disquieting reminder that the ordinary people of England were participants in this event: there were more regicides than those later punished at the Restoration.[11]

In historians like Echard and particularly Kennet, then, we experience the execution emotionally. To be sure, there is unfortunately no dearth of out-of-the-scene commentary, editorializing that to an extent spoils what could have been great art. We might wish that after his wonderful presentation of the terrifying scene on the scaffold, complete with hooks and staples, Echard had not seen fit to intrude that this sight could not daunt the king's "Christian or Royal Courage" (660), or that in his remarks on the same subject Kennet did not go on to insist that "by the Example of his Saviour, he resisted not, he disappointed their Wit, and yielded to their Malice" (3: 187). This kind of history is encumbered with the deadweight of overt didacticism. But even in spite of these limitations, there is still considerable power in the execution scenes of writers such as Echard and Kennet. By concentrating meaningful details, they make us feel the awful event; they place us uncomfortably close to the scaffold.

4

From the intimate historical narration we move to the other extreme, the narration that achieves its power through aesthetic distance. In the first we are immersed in the scene; in the second we step back and experience the scene as a stylized display within a frame, complete with its own special coloring and iconography.

Hume is the preeminent example of this manner, but before we look at Hume it is worthwhile to consider what has to be viewed as the ultimate in aesthetic distance: the treatment of Charles's beheading by that greatest of 17th-century English historians, Lord Clarendon. Clarendon's art is paradoxically the denial that art is possible. That is to say, when he comes to paint the scene, Clarendon lays down the brush and confesses himself unequal to proceed. In some detail he speaks of the king's ordeal at his trial and his "majestic behaviour," but in an expansive and grand periodic sentence he alludes to the awful event of regicide without being able to speak of it directly: thus "the most execrable murder that was ever committed since that of our blessed Saviour" is "so well known ... that the farther mentioning it in this place would but afflict and grieve the reader, and make the relation itself odious as well as needless."[12]

To be sure, all the allusive details in Clarendon's period do in fact suggest the dimensions of the tragedy at the same time that the historian denies that he can mention it. Thus Clarendon says more than he claims he can. Overall, however, Clarendon is exploiting the argument that the tragedy he must describe is unique. That tragic art or history painting can ennoble unspeakable suffering is a commonplace, yet here is a deed beyond the redemptive reach of art. Aesthetic distance is so great that we can barely perceive the execution. The historian implies that the event is somehow analogous only to the Crucifixion, and thus all the allusive meaning and impact of that central event in Western culture come flooding into Clarendon's narration.

Unlike the intimate account of White Kennet, we do not have to relive a presence on the scaffold. Rather we view a great and dignified statesman, loyal servant of the royal family, break down with grief at the image of the execution in his mind. But if Clarendon cannot speak directly of the execution, he can in a sense deliver a eulogy for the king that could not be given him after he died. With outrage Clarendon relates how the king's body finally was obscurely buried at Windsor Castle. The Puritan governor of the castle will not permit the use of the Book of Common Prayer, and the king finally has to be laid to rest in an almost makeshift place in the chapel, later so defaced and altered by Puritan zeal that no one could remember the location after the Restoration. "There the King's body was laid without any words, or other ceremonies than the tears and sighs of the few beholders. Upon the coffin was a plate of silver fixed with these words only, *King Charles 1648* [o.s.]" (3: 1: 342).

All along in Clarendon's narrative, the unbearable grief of the king's subjects becomes his lasting memorial. This final passage in Clarendon's character of the king fully testifies to that grief: "To conclude, he was the worthiest gentleman, the best master, the best friend, the best husband, the best father, and the best Christian, that the age in which he lived produced. And if he were not the greatest king, if he were without some parts and qualities which have made some kings great and happy, no other prince was ever unhappy who was possessed of half his virtues and endowments, and so much without any kind of vice" (3: 1: 340).

Clarendon's presentation, then, is actually a combination of the intimate and the remote styles. Hume says that Clarendon cannot speak of the execution, but that remark is not quite right. As we have seen, Clarendon manages to say a good deal about it while maintaining that he cannot bring himself to do so. In fact one could argue that the whole preparatory and concluding section on the king's end, framing the putative hiatus of the event, is focused on his execution in a way that we find in no other historian. Other royalists may bewail the king's fate and curse the regicides, but only in Clarendon do we find a first-hand supporter of the king remembering the end of the royal martyr with an emotion whose genuineness might be difficult to believe in any other writer.[13] The bloody spectacle has been removed entirely from view, while the "noble historian" himself takes center stage. Clarendon's handling of the execution is a brilliant example of the genre we have been considering.

5

Of all those who have treated the execution of Charles, David Hume is the only writer who also analyzed from a theoretical position the aesthetic possibilities and goals of such an endeavor. Like the French neoclassical critics whom he tends to echo, Hume characteristically deplores the blood and gore too prevalent on the English Renaissance stage, and in both theory and practice he favors aesthetic distance. This early statement in the *Treatise of Human Nature* (1739–40) is revealing: "Thus we find, that tho' every one, but especially women, are apt to contract a kindness for criminals, who go to the scaffold, and readily imagine them to be uncommonly handsome and well-shap'd; yet one, who is present at the cruel execution of the rack, feels no such tender emotions; but is in a manner overcome with horror, and has no leisure to temper this uneasy sensation by any opposite sympathy."[14] Hume appears to be saying that an execution scene has a great sympathetic potential, but only if certain conditions are met. The spectator tends to look favorably on the victim, but only if not overwhelmed by the trauma of the event—that is, by witnessing actual pain and suffering.[15] For the artist the actual execution itself cannot be a proper subject: prolonged anguish, for example, is simply brutal and horrifying. Rather, human behavior leading up to the execution is the focus of art.

Hume's most extended discussion of this problem is to be found in "Of Tragedy" (1757), an essay generally concerned with the question of why tragedy should exist as an art form at all — that is to say, how intrinsically unpleasant events can become beautiful through art. It was a problem that had intrigued other theorists, some of whom Hume treats in the essay, but for our purposes the direction that his discussion takes is of great interest. There are many subjects of tragedy, of course, but in Hume's mind the principal tragic scene is in fact an execution. Though he may briefly allude to other examples, as he does disapprovingly to the "shocking images" of bloodiness found too often "in ENGLISH theatre," Hume's central idea of tragedy is nevertheless that of a great hero triumphing over the inherent shame and horror of execution.[16]

The notion of triumph is all-important, for Hume specifically condemns painters for so frequently representing "such horrible subjects as crucifixions and martyrdoms, where nothing appears but tortures, wounds, executions, and passive suffering, without any action or affection." Further, in drama the "mere suffering of plaintive virtue, under the triumphant tyranny and oppression of vice, forms a disagreeable spectacle." Not "triumphant tyranny," but rather the triumph of goodness is what Hume demands. And so in successful tragedy the victim must either display "a noble courageous despair, or the vice receive its proper punishment" (224). Like many of his contemporaries, Hume may long for poetic justice, but if history is to be one's source of material, then providing the first satisfaction is easier than the second. We note, then, that Hume's tragic hero must not be acted on but rather dominate the scene, suffering with "a noble courageous despair." And whether disagreeable images can be converted into pleasure or rather will finally overpower that pleasure, the key lies in the hands of the teller of the story, the painter of the picture — in whatever medium, the artist. To be able to show that human anguish and despair can be made beautiful is the triumph of tragic art.

Hume's essay abounds in examples of what does not constitute genuine tragedy. On the other hand, almost the only example of a subject that would succeed as tragedy is, as it turns out, the execution of Charles I. This is what Hume says:

> Lord CLARENDON, when he approaches towards the catastrophe of the royal party, supposes, that his narration must then become infinitely disagreeable; and he hurries over the king's death, without giving us one circumstance of it. He considers it as too horrid a scene to be contemplated with any satisfaction, or even without the utmost pain and aversion. He himself, as well as the readers of that age, were too deeply concerned in the events, and felt a pain from subjects, which an historian and a reader of another age would regard as the most pathetic and most interesting [i.e., emotionally involving], and, by consequence, the most agreeable. (223–24)

Before, we noted Hume's assumption that being too close to the actuality of suffering itself would negate a sympathetic response, and here we see that this undesirable closeness can even be defined in terms of an audience's relationship to those involved. Instead of people we know, the participants must be dramatis personae. Once again, art depends upon distance. But given that distance, no subject strikes Hume as more suitable for tragic art than the fate of Charles.

Of course by the time Hume wrote "Of Tragedy" he had already completed his own version of this best of tragic subjects, for the reign of Charles I had appeared three years before in the first volume (1754) of his *History of England*. In letters to friends he confesses that his portrayal of Charles is intentionally emotional, and he also sees it as a tragic theme to be rendered by art: "I did indeed endeavour to paint the King's Catastrophe . . . in as pathetic a manner as I cou'd."[17] And late in his life Hume remembers the *History* primarily in terms of his treatment of the king, for he is the man "who had presumed to shed a generous tear for the fate of Charles I."[18] Let us see how Hume handles the denouement of this tragedy.

Proper distance is the key to appreciating Hume's version. More than a century had given him and his readers sufficient distance to make the participants in the event dramatis personae, not people in their own lives, but Hume and his readers were still near enough to the political, social, cultural—indeed the mythic—dimensions of the event to give it a power that we could never appreciate. And Hume makes sure that the other kind of distance, the aesthetic, is achieved through a careful handling of detail. His readers see with blinding clarity the principals as symbolic figures, while details of distracting realism never appear in his great history painting.

I observed earlier that the theoretical Hume believes that the source of tragic power lies in the sublime stature of the hero—and thus in his victory over adversity as he faces death—and not at all in the details of execution. Hume the artist follows the formula exactly. Previously in the account of the king's life and afterwards in his character sketch, Hume's Charles comes across as at best "a good, rather than ... a great man" (5: 542). In the "last scene of his life," however, Charles is given a greater script: "he never forgot his part, either as a prince or as a man.... His soul, without effort or affectation, seemed only to remain in the situation familiar to it, and to look down with contempt on all the efforts of human malice and iniquity" (5: 537). And then, through long passages leading up to the execution itself, Hume fashions the king into his own exemplary tragic hero. Despite insults and jeers, Charles remains superior to his antagonists. He even manages to sleep soundly while carpenters hammer away on his scaffold.

It is important to stress that this heroic Charles is largely Hume's creation. Hume takes hints in his sources and magnifies or embroiders them, and the sources that he uses most are those that are most fervently Royalist and hence least reliable. Take, for example, this passage, with its transparent pathos: "The people, though under the rod of lawless, unlimited power, could not forbear, with the most ardent prayers, pouring forth their wishes for his preservation; and, in his present distress, they avowed *him*, by their generous tears, for their monarch, whom, in their misguided fury, they had before so violently rejected. The king was softened at this moving scene, and expressed his gratitude for their dutiful affection" (5: 537–38). "This moving scene," one suspects from examining all the evidence, existed more in Hume's imagination than it ever did in reality. Hume seizes a hint from Richard Perrinchief's significantly titled *Royal Martyr* and rolls the drums ominously to stir the "great passions":[19] "The people remained in that silence and astonishment which all great passions, when they have not an opportunity of exerting themselves, naturally produce in the human mind" (5: 538). As to the claim that Charles could have heard workmen building his scaffold, most contemporary sources attest that Charles slept some distance away at St. James's, not near the scaffold at Whitehall, but Hume cites Clement Walker's largely fanciful account as his authority. In fact, however, Hume manages even to outdo Walker, for even that ardent Royalist does not claim specifically that Charles had the heroic fortitude to sleep despite the noise: only that "this was a new device to mortifie him, but it would not do."[20]

In all these constructions Hume is manifestly determined that his Charles be no passive martyr, that infinitely suffering thing so much maligned in "Of Tragedy." To be sure, Charles himself had assumed the epithet "Martyr" at his end, a title which after the Restoration had become quasi-official, not only among his partisans but even throughout the Church of England. Hume flirts with the possibility of Charles as martyr or even Christ, recording that "he forgave all his enemies, even the chief instruments of his death" (5: 540). And after the execution itself, Hume indulges in a long passage recording the cataclysmic reaction to the awesome event, reminiscent of the Crucifixion:

> It is impossible to describe the grief, indignation, and astonishment, which took place . . . throughout the whole nation, as soon as the report of this fatal execution was conveyed to them. . . . Women are said to have cast forth the untimely fruit of their womb: Others fell into convulsions, or sunk into such a melancholy as attended them to their grave: Nay some, unmindful of themselves, as though they could not, or would not survive their beloved prince, it is reported, suddenly fell down dead. (5: 540–41)

Hume takes this astounding information almost verbatim from Perrinchief, though it is also found in other similarly "inspired" versions.[21] Apparently Hume is attempting so hard to be the artist that he forgets his more customary philosophical skepticism: he is, after all, famous for his masterful refutation of the possibility of miracles in the *Enquiry concerning Human Understanding* (1748).[22] Hume thus seems ready to exploit special effects that will heighten the impact of the great tragedy, at least as he conceived of tragedy. Overall, however, despite these uses of the "martyr" tradition, Hume's Charles emerges more as dominating hero than sacrificial lamb.[23]

The beheading itself is the critical scene in the drama. Hume demonstrates how an execution can be handled in the grand style. He notes the regicides' intention that the location of the scaffold – that is, placed before Whitehall – would symbolically "display . . . the triumph of popular justice over royal majesty." That intention, of course, is to prove vain, for Hume's scene is resplendent with an overwhelming sense of royal majesty. Charles steps onto the scaffold, sees that he cannot be heard by the multitude, and hence addresses "the few persons who were about him; particularly colonel Tomlinson, to whose care he had lately been committed, and upon whom, as upon many others, his amiable deportment had wrought an entire conversion" (5: 540). So complete is the king's command of the scene that even those charged with the task of killing him, it would seem, nonetheless love him – an impression, we might note, that is largely invented for artistic purposes. Hume gives us only the gist of the king's last speech, one suspects because a dignified paraphrase is more ideal than direct discourse. Hume thus replaces the frail man at his final hour with a timeless figure of sublime power speaking to an elite audience convoked by art.

Indeed Hume is determined that no sign of weakness or passivity be evident, as we see in the actual moment of execution:

> When he was preparing himself for the block, bishop Juxon called to him: "There is, Sir, but one stage more, which, though turbulent and troublesome, is yet a very short one. Consider, it will soon carry you a great way; it will carry you from earth to heaven; and there you shall find, to your great joy, the prize to which you hasten, a crown of glory." "I go," replied the king, "from a corruptible to an incorruptible crown; where no disturbance can have place." At one blow was his head severed from his body. A man in a vizor performed the office of executioner: Another, in a like disguise, held up to the spectators, the head, streaming with blood, and cried aloud, *This is the head of a traitor!* (5: 540).

Consider what has been left out: all the delays concerning the fastness and height of the block, the positioning of the hair, the disrobing, the sign; the request that the king not be put to pain; the scaffold draped in black and the staples. In some respects these details would be distractions from the single focus of Hume's painting. More importantly, however, they would shift the balance of power away from the king to the malign forces attempting to punish him. Dignity, confidence, and strength must instead be embodied in the king; otherwise there is no hero.

One might object that at the end an executioner does hold up the king's bloody head to view, announcing that justice has been dealt a traitor. Hence royal majesty is defeated at last. But not so. The severed head suddenly shocks the reader, as it does the spectators, with the enormity of what has happened, and as symbol it sets off the cataclysm of reaction noted earlier. Judgment is preponderantly against those who have dared to kill their king. Indeed, the whole world is shaken and outraged. Hence in addition to a hero with noble courage, Hume has that other satisfaction of tragedy, poetic justice, as vice receives "its proper punishment."

Admittedly, in his striving for the sublime Hume may end up with a performance that we may find too stiff, affected, and patently manipulated. His execution is artificial in the older sense of a word that in Hume's day was complimentary, but in ours, pejorative. Precisely those details he omits in the execution are what give the account of White Kennet its immediacy and impact. Even when Hume does present a touching, human scene—for example, when the king bids his youngest children farewell—he paraphrases too much of it. Compare Kennet's version of Charles's last words to his daughter Elizabeth with Hume's: (1) "He bid her tell her Mother, that *his Thoughts had never strayed from her, and that his Love should be the same to the last*" (185); (2) "the king gave her in charge to tell the queen, that during the whole course of his life, he had never once, even in thought, failed in his fidelity towards her; and that his conjugal tenderness and his life should have an equal duration" (5: 539). The difference between Kennet and Hume is that while Kennet is presenting a true drama, Hume instead is painting a grand picture, or projecting emblematic tableaux. On the scaffold we see the emblem of royal majesty, not a man.

Hume's success, however, in his own day can be measured not only by the number of contemporary tributes—or even by the fact that Louis XVI selected Hume's account to read in the days before his own beheading[24]—but also in the version of a historian who set out to answer Hume's supposedly Tory account, Catherine Macaulay's *History of England*, whose story of Charles I appeared in 1768. Although

Macaulay grants that in his death Charles exhibited "the magnanimity of heroism and the patience of martyrdom" (415), she does all she can to remind her reader that he was nonetheless an evil king. In the following remark she may very well have been thinking of the response that Hume encourages: "To a mind softened by habits of amusement, and intoxicated with ideas of self-importance, the transition from royal pomp to a prison, from easy, gay, and luxurious life to a premature and violent death by the hands of an executioner, are punishments so sharp and touching, that, in the suffering prince, we are apt to overlook the designing tyrant, to dwell on his hardships, and forget his crimes" (417–18). And in her own version of the execution she seems to be consciously opposing Hume's highly charged presentation. Hers is a flat, humdrum paraphrase of Hume's, even introducing elements of burlesque to divest the scene of its Humean majesty:

> Whilst he was preparing for execution, the bishop poured out a few insipid lifeless exhortations: To these the King returned, "I go from a corruptible to an incorruptible crown, where no disturbance can have place." Then laying his head upon the block, the executioner (whose face was concealed in a vizor) severed it with one stroke from the body: an assistant (in like disguise) held it up to the spectators, streaming with blood, and after the usual manner observed in similar executions, cried aloud, "This is the head of a traitor." (416–17)

The bishop's attendance here is sufficiently inept, but his presence is even more of a liability when we consider that, when he is introduced a few lines before, Macaulay terms him "a cold inanimate speaker" whom the king had nonetheless requested. And she interrupts the great scene with a long footnote detailing the bishop's farcical consternation at being summoned—"'God save me! what a trick is this that I should have no more warning'"—and his desperate recourse to an old sermon and a feckless celebration of the sacrament (416n).[25] From Macaulay's point of view, Hume's compelling art required a strongly opposing dose of anti-art.

As we have seen, then, historical versions of the execution of Charles I run through the spectrum of aesthetic possibility—from realistic to stylized, from close-range to distant, from dramatic to painterly, indeed from ridiculous to sublime. But however they handled the material, the historians of that event were simply responding to an assumption that executions typically contained an inherent aesthetic. Samuel Y. Edgerton, Jr., observes: "Public execution probably reached its apogee of artful performance during the 16th century.... The beheading of Charles I ... was one of the last grand public executions in the medieval pageant tradition.... The very performance of beheading lent itself to esthetics." If, as Edgerton argues, "public execution not only survived under the impact of Renaissance humanism but even thrived in the guise of art"[26]—and by "art" he means the ritualistic symbolism of execution itself and the genre of painting that enjoyed a symbiosis with it—then it is no wonder that 17th- and 18th-century historiography should have attempted to give the death of Charles aesthetic form. In an historian like Hume, the life and death of this unfortunate king could be perceived and accordingly presented in no other terms than as a perfect tragedy.

Notes

I wish to thank the University of South Carolina both for a Research and Productive Scholarship Grant and for sabbatical leave that enabled me to complete the research and writing of this essay.

1. Laurence Echard, *The History of England*, 3d ed. (London, 1720), 660–61; subsequent citations are from this text.

2. Bishop Gilbert Burnet calls "that great transaction ... one of the most amazing scenes in history"; see *Burnet's History of His Own Time* (London, 1766), 1: 63. Later, while the Whiggish John Oldmixon ridicules Echard's overblown account—"*Echard* always over does every Thing"—Oldmixon is forced to admit, even when condemning Charles, "But I am too much mov'd with writing the tragical Scene to have any such ungenerous Sentiments toward a suffering Prince." See Oldmixon's *History of England* (London, 1730), 369; subsequent citations are from this text.

3. For an interesting study of the function of executions in the Puritan drama of repentant sinners, see Daniel E. Williams, "'Behold a Tragick Scene Strangely Changed into a Theater of Mercy': The Structure and Significance of Criminal Conversion Narratives in Early New England," *American Quarterly* 38 (1986): 827–47.

4. Oldmixon devotes a good part of his *History* to exposing the so-called errors of historians such as Clarendon and especially Echard. He censures Echard's delight in revenge (370, 478, 485) and concludes, "After Echard has seen all these Sufferers ript up and mangled, he performs the last Office [Echard was an archdeacon], and kills them in their Characters" (486). Clement Walker in his *Compleat History of Independencie* (London, 1661) is an early example of detailed delight in the extermination of "those infernal Regicides" (part 3, 114).

5. *The History of England*, 6 vols. (1754–62; rpt. Indianapolis, Ind.: Liberty Classics, 1983), 6: 162. All subsequent citations of Hume's *History* are from this text.

6. See, for example, J. C. Hilson, "Hume: The Historian as Man of Feeling," in *Augustan Worlds*, ed. J. C. Hilson et al. (Bristol, England: Leicester University Press, 1978), 205–22; also see my essay "The Sentimental Sublime in Hume's *History of England*," *Review of English Studies* n.s. 40 (August 1989): 350–72, and chapter 1 of my book, *The Moral Animus of David Hume*. (Newark, Del.: University of Delaware Press, 1990).

7. See, for example, the recent discussion of the subject in Hayden White, *The Content of the Form: Narrative Discourse and Historical Representation* (Baltimore: Johns Hopkins University Press, 1987).

8. Quotations of Rushworth and Whitelock are from these editions: John Rushworth, *Historical Collections* (London, 1721); Bulstrode Whitelock, *Memorials of the English Affairs* (Oxford: Oxford University Press, 1853).

9. Whitelock at least inserts this sentence between the mention of the blow and the coffin: "The king died with true magnanimity and Christian patience" (2: 516). In that respect his almost perfunctory attempt to moralize the scene goes a small way past the barer chronicle of Rushworth.

10. [White Kennet], *A Complete History of England*, 2d ed. (London, 1719), 3: 185; subsequent citations are from this text.

11. Kennet also observes in a footnote that the identity of the executioners was never discovered, though he was told of a dying butcher who desperately sent his daughter for a clergyman to confess to, but who died unshriven (3: 187n).

12. *The History of the Rebellion and Civil Wars in England* (Oxford: Clarendon Press, 1816), 3: 1: 337; subsequent citations are from this text.

13. In her excellent study of Clarendon, Martine Watson Brownley points out that great scenes are not Clarendon's métier because he disliked and distrusted rhetoric in history, preferring analysis instead; nonetheless, his strong emotions occasionally overcame his reserve, particularly regarding the king's end: "Rhetorical denunciation heavily colors his portrayal of the last days of Charles I." See *Clarendon and the Rhetoric of Historical Form* (Philadelphia: University of Pennsylvania Press, 1985), 39, 42–43.

14. *A Treatise of Human Nature*, ed. L. A. Selby-Bigge (Oxford: Clarendon Press, 1888), 388.

15. In a somewhat similar vein, Michel Foucault has considered the effects on spectators of actual executions in *Discipline and Punish: The Birth of the Prison*, trans. Alan Sheridan (New York: Vintage Books, 1979), 9, 59–61, et passim. Concerning the aesthetic problem Hume is analyzing here, one might also think of Lessing's fundamental contention in *Laokoon* (1766) that the static image of extreme suffering can never be beautiful.

16. *Essays, Moral, Political, and Literary*, ed. Eugene F. Miller (Indianapolis, Ind.: Liberty Classics, 1985), 224; subsequent citations are from this text.

17. *The Letters of David Hume*, ed. J. Y. T. Greig (Oxford: Clarendon Press, 1932), 1: 222; see also 1: 47.

18. *Essays*, xxxvii.

19. *The Royal Martyr: or, The Life and Death of King Charles I* (London, 1676), 198–99; subsequent citations are from this text.

20. Walker, part 2, 110. David Lloyd in *Memoires* . . . (London, 1668), 214, repeats the story, but to my knowledge no other contemporary makes the claim. Hilson also makes the point that in this case Hume is obviously "tampering with historical fact" (215). Not long after Hume's account, Catherine Macaulay angrily rebutted this "calumny on the parliament" propagated by "Clement Walker, a petulant writer of the Presbyterian party." See her *History of England* (London, 1763–83), 4: 415n; subsequent citations of Macaulay are from this text.

21. Note how close Hume is to the passage in Perrinchief: "When the news of his Death was divulged, Women with Child for grief cast forth the untimely Fruit of the Womb. . . . Others, both Men and Women, fell into Convulsions and swounding Fits, and contracted so deep a Melancholy as attended them to the Grave. Some unmindful of themselves, as though they could not, or would not, live when their beloved Prince was slaughtered, (it is reported) suddenly fell down dead" (211). Lloyd (220), William Sanderson, *A Compleat History of* . . . *King Charles* (London, 1658), 1139, and as we have already seen at the beginning of this essay, Echard, 661, all include similar passages, though Hume's phrasing is closest to Perrinchief's.

22. Oldmixon scoffs at these miracles (369–70), and it is a gauge of Hume's artistic purposes that the great skeptic himself should repeat these stories.

23. Some Royalists, of course, did portray Charles as the Lamb of God. Perrinchief goes so far as to capitalize all pronouns referring to Charles and describes the beheading as an act of sacrilege: "having His Eyes and Hands like fore-runners lifted up to Heaven, . . . He kneeled down to the Block as at a Desk of Prayer, and meekly submitted His *Crowned Head* to the pleasure of His God, to be profaned by the Axe of the disguised

Executioner" (205). Both Sanderson (1138) and Lloyd (220) say the king knelt as at a prayer-desk. Sir William Dugdale in *A Short View of the Late Troubles in England* (London, 1681) says that Charles "meekly submitted to the stroke of the Axe" (373). A century later the Whiggish Catherine Macaulay protests the tendency among Royalist historians "ridiculously and impiously" to vilify the regicides even more than "the crucifiers of their God" (4: 426).

24. See J. B. A. Clèry, *Journal de ce qui s'est passé a la tour du Temple pendant la captivité de Louis XVI, Roi de France* (London, 1798), 203; quoted in Laurence L. Bongie, *David Hume: Prophet of the Counter-Revolution* (Oxford: Clarendon Press, 1965), 125–26.

25. Macaulay's depiction of the bishop is basically a slur, for most sources praise his abilities and judgment—even the Puritans could find no fault in him—and her source is Edmund Ludlow, a writer not to be regarded as objective.

26. "*Maniera* and the *Mannaia*: Decorum and Decapitation in the Sixteenth Century," in *The Meaning of Mannerism*, ed. Franklin W. Robinson and Stephen G. Nichols, Jr. (Hanover, N.H.: University Press of New England, 1972), 67, 87, 69.

Locke and Beccaria: Faculty Psychology and Capital Punishment

STEVEN LYNN

The Italian critic who called Cesare Beccaria's *Trattato dei delitti e delle pene* (Essay on crimes and punishments) "indisputably the most effective literary work of the entire eighteenth century" may perhaps be forgiven his enthusiasm, for the international influence of Beccaria's work, published in July 1764, and translated almost immediately into every major language, appears to have been enormous. By 1822 it was possible for Beccaria's Paris editor to credit him with "the abolition of torture in most European states, the suppression of cruel punishments, and the improvement of penal law."[1] Modern assessments have agreed without exception that Beccaria "inspired far-reaching reforms in criminal law" and helped shape the thinking of a host of 18th century thinkers, ranging from Benjamin Franklin to Voltaire.[2] Yet, in reading through the history of criminal law and punishment, one notes with dismay that in England it was not until 1789 that the last execution by burning was carried out; not until 1834 that branding as a punishment was abolished; not until 1837 that the pillory was outlawed; and not until 1820 that the number of capital crimes begins to decrease, having gone from less than fifty in Tudor and Stuart times to more than two hundred.[3] If Beccaria's work is, as Harry Barnes says, "the most effective work in the field of the reform of criminal jurisprudence" (not as extravagant a claim perhaps as "the most effective literary work," but certainly a substantial assertion), its effectiveness may well seem slow and limited nonetheless.[4] To be sure, Beccaria's profound reluctance to employ capital punishment was often echoed and invoked in the 18th and 19th centuries; and, in England in the period 1803–1810, for example, of 1,872 thieves convicted and sentenced to death, only one was actually executed.[5] But, as Leon Radzinowicz points out in his massive *History of English Criminal Law*, replacing capital punishment with imprisonment was often replacing a quick and relatively painless death with a slow, torturous one, given the conditions of imprisonment. Moreover, Radzinowicz argues, Beccaria's reforms were severely compromised because his focus on capital punishment "neglected the problem of secondary punishments, without the solution of which any reform of criminal law was destined to remain abortive."[6]

Although there is no doubt some truth in Radzinowicz's observation, Beccaria does not entirely neglect secondary punishments, for he does provide insistently a governing principle for all punishments: they should "make the strongest and most lasting impressions on the minds of others, with the least torment to the body of the criminal" (41–42). Beccaria's qualified success or qualified failure (whichever one prefers) is, I would argue, more complex than a neglect or focus on this or that particular facet of crime and punishment. To understand more fully why Beccaria was accorded such immediate and continued applause, and why, given this pervasive appreciation of Beccaria, his practical impact was not more radical and precipitous, we need to understand better the intellectual context his work inhabited. Most often Beccaria has been considered as a point of origin, a context for later developments, and when Beccaria's own contexts have been considered, the effort has been primarily to track down the genealogy of various progressive ideas.[7] I propose here an investigation of what is in some ways a more fundamental, yet neglected, relationship: how does the model of the mind that Beccaria and his contemporaries inherited influence the genesis and reception of his ideas? Eighteenth century assumptions about the workings of the mind, I will suggest, help to explain both Beccaria's spectacular intellectual appeal as well as the incomplete and glacially slow response to his ideas in practice.[8]

If we want some idea of how Beccaria and others in the 18th century might have viewed the mind, Locke's *Essay concerning Human Understanding*, evolved in the 1670s and 1680s, published in 1690, would seem to be the logical document to examine. Throughout this period, according to Kenneth MacLean, Locke's work had the most influence of any book, the Bible only excepted; W. S. Howell agrees that Locke's works on understanding "were without question the most popular, the most widely read, the most frequently reprinted, and the most influential of all English books."[9] It is not surprising then that Locke's model of the mind pervades 18th century thought. To choose only one example, Beccaria's friend, Helvetius, uses Locke's theory of mind to found his notions of man's equality.[10] Thus, to understand Beccaria, we need to consider how Locke constructs his psychology, and what its essence is—not in order to demonstrate that Beccaria employed Locke specifically, but rather to consider the implications of the psychology Beccaria and his age would have assumed.

Locke's principal tools of analysis in constructing his model of the mind are erasure and deformation.[11] Seeing himself as an "Under-Labourer," "clearing Ground a little, and removing some of the rubbish that lies in the way to Knowledge," Locke considers what our understanding would be like if we could not see, if our senses were quicker, if two souls occupied the same body, if a cat and a rat mated.[12] His most famous erasure, the subject of Book I, removed innate ideas, thus requiring that the materials our minds manipulate must ultimately derive from sensations. Sensations must act upon something, and so Locke implies a mental surface that receives the impress of sensations; then he considers what it would be like to erase this surface, to return to that preinfantile state of the famous *tabula rasa*. He also imagines an organ or system for thought, and how this biological thinking machine would function if it too were returned to an original, blank state. In order to work, the mind would need various capacities, or "faculties," that this empty mind must have in order to function. By "faculties," Locke tells us, he does not mean "some real Beings in the Soul" or "so many distinct Agents in us"—alarming ideas (237); rather, he means only a power or an ability (241).

In his qualification of "faculties," Locke is attempting to avoid the kind of explanatory regress that answers the question "What digested the groceries?" with the response "The digestive faculty." But by saying that a faculty is not an agent but rather a power, Locke is nonetheless unable to avoid the implication of a partitioned mind, composed of separate functions—a model that displaces the problem of "mind" rather than explaining it, for the simple reason that some entity, some personhood, would seem necessarily to be in charge of the various faculties. Hence, we see the necessity and the attractiveness of positing a soul that receives and superintends the operations of the faculties. But Locke is not willing to situate this soul in a particular place, unlike Descartes and others who favor the pineal gland as its home; in fact, Locke is not willing to give the soul materiality at all, but at the same time he is equally unwilling to assign it immateriality: "'Tis past controversy, that we have in us something that thinks; our very Doubts about what it is confirm the certainty of its being, though we must content our selves in the Ignorance of what kind of *Being* it is."[13]

This displacement of the mind's agency and the ambiguous status of its nature allow Locke's model of the mind to serve his thesis well, for a crucial aspect of Locke's project involves exposing the extent to which the mind is a passive receptacle for sensations: by exposing the gap between these sensations and our ideas, especially our complex ideas (or "notions" Locke would prefer) like "murder" and "sacrilege," Locke hopes to promote tolerance and humility: "The necessity of believing, without Knowledge, nay, often upon very slight grounds, in this fleeting state of Action and Blindness we are in, should make us more busy and careful to inform our selves, than constrain others" (660). This drive toward toleration and generosity is also fostered by Locke's discussion "Of the Imperfection of Words," the title of chapter 9 in Book III. Because words cannot cross this gap between sensations and thoughts, Locke insists that words "*stand for nothing but the* Ideas *in the Mind of him that uses them,* how imperfectly soever or carelessly those *Ideas* are collected from the things which they are supposed to represent" (405; emphasis is Locke's). Among those words exemplifying the "arbitrary imposition" (478) of meaning, Locke includes "Justice, Just; Equality, Equal" (474).

Beccaria, near the outset of his treatise, similarly undermines his contemporaries' confidence in the word "justice," informing them "We should be cautious how we associate with the word *justice*, an idea of any thing real, such as a physical power, or a being that actually exists" (9). By acknowledging, like Locke, the gap between *res* and *verba*, Beccaria reminds us that "justice" is an arbitrary construct, which for him means "nothing more, than that bond which is necessary to keep the interest of individuals united" (9). This move dismantles for Beccaria the institutionalized conception of "justice" as a stable standard, grounded in reality—a conception that involved retribution in the idea of justice, and led to such absurdities as trying and executing animals and even insects. It was this need to balance some evil with retribution and purgation in order to realize "justice" that led, for example, the French legal system in 1386 to try, sentence, torture, and execute by hanging a pig that had injured a young boy.[14] Such a ritualistic approach to punishment survives well into the 18th century with the procession to Tyburn, or the practice in aggravated cases of returning the criminal to the crime's scene for his punishment. Beccaria and other enlightened 18th century thinkers reject an economy of justice that requires an injury to be offset by an equal injury.

"Justice" is not the only term that Beccaria writes under erasure. All complex words, he says in Lockean language, are composed of "simple ideas" that are "easily confounded"—which explains why "truths of morality" are less distinctly known than "the revolutions of the heavenly bodies" (32). As examples, Beccaria points to "the uncertainty of our notions of honour and virtue," an uncertainty made inevitable by the arbitrary connnection between "names" and "the things they originally signified" (23). Beccaria, tacitly following Locke, is so much aware of the prisonhouse of language that he would have no one placed in a more substantial prisonhouse on the basis of words: "when the question relates to the words of a criminal," "the credibility of a witness is null." Actions, *res*, must found an accusation, not *verba*—which, as Locke tells us, "stand for nothing but the *Ideas* in the Mind of him that uses them."

Thus, Locke's description of the mind's fundamental faculty establishes this position, crucial to his argument as well as Beccaria's: "the first faculty of the Mind" is "bare naked *Perception*," which is "the inlet of all Knowledge,"; in the performance of this faculty, "the Mind is, for the most part, only passive" (149, 143)—Locke will later say the mind, "in respect to its simple *Ideas*, is wholly passive" (288). The ambiguous status—where is it? what is it?—of the "something that thinks" tends to accentuate the primacy of sensations and the passivity of the mind. This passivity, together with the arbitrariness of words (which is built on the apparent happenstance of sensation), presents a model of the mind conducive to forgiveness, not harsh punishment: we are shaped by our environments, by the sensations we receive and the actions of our faculties upon these sensations. And because of the imperfection of words, and the lack of innate ideas, including the absence of an innate moral code, our convictions (in both senses) should be suspect and tentative.

Beccaria's humanitarian outlook is thus based on assumptions that obviously accord with Locke's model of perception. Beccaria takes for granted, for example, that our ideas are based on our sensations: while the legal system in his day presumed the accused to be guilty and forced him to prove his innocence, Beccaria argues, based tacitly on Lockean psychology, that the presumption should be against the accuser, "for no man is cruel [that is, in accusing another of a serious crime] without some motive of fear or hate. There are no spontaneous or superfluous sentiments in the heart of man; they are the result of impressions on the senses" (45). Similarly, Beccaria's argument against the practice of using torture to extract the truth is based on the following premise: "Every act of the will is invariably in proportion to the force of the impression on our senses; and the sensibility of every man is limited" (60). If a man's ideas are completely occupied at the fundamental level by pain, he is not likely to tell the truth; he is only likely to tell whatever will end the pain.

Beccaria's extraordinary reluctance to invoke capital punishment, or any extreme punishment, is also related to the perceiver's passivity in Locke's model. Because our sentiments are "all the result of impressions on the senses" (45), Beccaria is especially reluctant to punish harshly those crimes that obviously result from the criminal's environment and experiences. For example, punishing sodomy with torture and severe punishment, including capital punishment, seems outrageous to him because the crime is the result not so much of "the passions of man" as the present system of education, in which "ardent youth are carefully excluded from all commerce with the other sex, as the vigour of nature blooms" (125). Indeed, in all crimes Beccaria tends to see the perpetrator as another victim, driven to do wrong by what he has experienced. Robbery "alas! is commonly the effect of misery and despair" (80), he says for example. Beccaria in fact goes so far as to argue that the punishment of any crime cannot be just if the state has not endeavored by the best available means to prevent it (118).

Beccaria shares with a number of 18th century reformers this willingness to imagine sympathetically the thought processes of the criminal (and potential criminal). Samuel Johnson, to quote only one illustrious example quoting another illustrious example, in *Rambler* 114 confirms Boerhaave's remark "that he never saw a criminal dragged to execution without asking himself, 'Who knows whether this man is not less culpable than me?'"[15] Such empathy, which becomes more and more common as the age of reason becomes the age of sensibility, certainly owes something to Locke's influence; and the idea that our minds work in the same ways, and this working is not entirely under our control, certainly tends to foster Boerhaave's sort of consideration. As Johnson writes in Sermon 26, perhaps revealing more of his own conscience than he intended, "scarce any one can see" a convicted thief "in the hands of the executioner, without reflecting that the crimes, for which they dye are less than his own."[16]

If Locke's description of the first faculty tends to suggest to his readers how anyone, shaped by his perceptions, might go astray, it is his discussion of the second faculty, retention, that actually gives a much deeper insight into the workings of deviance, and even madness. The implications of this second faculty also appear to strengthen our sympathy for the criminal/victim; but at the same time, pursued to their logical end, its implications finally underscore the necessity of punishment — even severe punishment, even (perhaps) capital punishment, despite our psychologically grounded sympathy.

The second faculty in Locke's model of the mind, "retention," or memory, allows us to store sensations in order to compare, relate, combine, discriminate, abstract, etc. This storage has its own problems, as "there seems to be a constant decay of all our Ideas, even of those which are struck deepest, and in Minds the most retentive" (151). Thus, if our ideas are not "sometimes renewed by repeated Exercise of the Senses, or Reflection on those kind of Objects, which at first occasioned them, the Print wears out, and at last there remains nothing to be seen" (151). Beccaria obviously employs a similar model of thinking when he notes that "ideas of morality are stamped on our minds by repeated impressions" (106). Unlawful acts become potentially failures of morality that are arguably the fault of the society, which fails to write its moral code on its citizens clearly enough or which allows its code to be naturally erased by neglect. Lacking an innate moral code, requiring "repeated exercise of the senses" in order to sustain an idea, human beings confront a fragile and even arbitrary system of right and wrong, as Beccaria stresses: "Whoever reads with a philosophic eye, the history of nations, and their laws, will generally find, that the ideas of virtue and vice, of a good or a bad citizen, change with the ages; not in proportion to the alteration of circumstances, and consequently conformable to the common good; but in proportion to the passions and errors by which the different law-givers were successively influenced" (23). This remark, which must be unsettling to anyone who would enforce the current laws with any ferocity, is followed by an even more disarming one, asserting that in fact "the passions and vices of one age, are the foundation of the morality of the following." This moral topsy-turviness results, Beccaria makes clear, from the way our sensations, impressions, passions, are "weakened by time."

If the imperfection of words and the fragility of ideas do tend toward empathy and leniency toward criminals, there is another aspect of this second faculty of retention that would appear to compel society to punish those who do wrong, despite its sympathy for them. This aspect is the association of whatever ideas we *are* able to retain and manipulate. Because we cannot work with a multitude of primary or "simple" ideas, as Locke explains, relationships between and among ideas are inevitably and necessarily formed as a function of thinking. Some of these associations, he says, are "natural" or real and therefore valuable. But, "there is another Connexion of *Ideas* wholly owing to Chance or Custom; *Ideas* that in themselves are not at all of kin, come to be so united in Mens Minds, that 'tis very hard to separate them" (395). This accidental association is not only a problem; it is, Locke thinks, "the foundation of the greatest" if not "all the Errors in the World" (401) – an astonishingly broad indictment. For Locke, however, such accidental associations, which occur with distressing frequency, engender an unreality, a kind of madness even, and he points to the unfounded yet irreconcilable and often violent oppositions between "different Sects of Philosophy and Religion" and "Party" as a prime example of the power (and danger) of association. With the second faculty, the mind, so passive in the workings of the first faculty, becomes disturbingly alive.

The plasticity of associations provides a logical basis for punishment, even harsh punishment, as a deterrent. In fact, Beccaria sees such deterrence as essential to the life of society, which

> is prevented from approaching to that dissolution (to which, as well as all other parts of the physical and moral world, it naturally tends) only by motives that are the immediate objects of sense, and which being continually presented to the mind, are sufficient to counterbalance the effect of the passions of the individual, which oppose the general good. Neither the power of eloquence nor the sublimest truths, are sufficient to restrain, for any length of time, those passions which are excited by the lively impressions of present objects. (6)

Such pessimism, which immediately strikes one as Hobbesian, can also be traced to Locke, who thinks it would be "utterly in vain" to propose a law without rewards and punishments (351). Servan, who refers enthusiastically to Beccaria's essay only three years after its publication, reveals how deterrence comes to be seen in terms of Lockean psychology, writing that "the immutable base of the strongest empires rests upon the soft fibres of the brain," and "to establish an association of ideas" to deter criminal acts, "there must be a regular association of events: in brief, the citizenry must see crimes punished always *as soon as they are committed.*"[17] Although Beccaria is more cautious than his adherent, raising the issue of justice miscarrying in the "promptitude of punishment," he considers the temporal connection of crime to punishment so important, being "one of the most powerful means of preventing crimes" (115), that the dangers of miscarriage are outweighed, and therefore crimes should be punished as soon as possible — if not "as soon as they are commited." Here is Beccaria, employing obviously Lockean language, even referring indirectly to Locke's *Essay* it appears, to explain the role of association in deterrence:

> An immediate punishment is more useful; because the smaller the interval of time between the punishment and the crime, the stronger and more lasting will be the association of the two ideas of Crime and Punishment; so that they may be considered, one as the cause, the other as the unavoidable and necessary effect. It is demonstrated, that the association of ideas is the cement which unites the fabric of the human intellect; without which, pleasure and pain would be simple and ineffectual sensations. (73–74)

When time elapses between the crime and punishment, Beccaria notes, the spectators see the punishment as "a terrible sight" rather than "the necessary consequence of a crime" (75), and deterrence is weakened.

Thus, the role of association in deterrence not only supports a rush to sentencing and punishment, it also makes severe, horrible punishment seem reasonable, for the more dramatic the associated deterrent, the more powerfully persons may be dissuaded from crime. If punishments were sufficiently horrible, one may reason, then no one in his or her right mind would break the law. Such logic led William Paley, who assumed with Beccaria and others that "The proper end of human punishment is not the satisfaction of justice but the prevention of crimes," to speculate soberly in 1785 on the possibility of beneficially augmenting "the horror of punishment" by "casting murderers into a den of wild beasts, where they would perish in a manner dreadful to the imagination, yet concealed from the view."[18] The check on such a not uncommon train of thought is expressed by Beccaria, once more working in terms of Lockean psychology: "In proportion as punishments become more cruel, the minds of men, as a fluid rises to the same height as that which surrounds it, grow hardened and insensible" (96). Such a hydraulic comparison, especially effective given the fluid mechanics of the nervous system as Locke and the medicine of his day understood it, might not apply to punishments not witnessed by the public, but only related to them. Hence Paley's stipulation, "concealed from the view."

This sort of thinking, supported powerfully by Locke's treatment of association, is arguably behind the widespread endorsement in Beccaria's day and even our own of capital punishment. And it is not enough, as Fielding argues in his *Enquiry into the Causes of the Late Increase of Robbers* (1751), to legislate capital punishment, and even to sentence persons to die; if the wrongdoers are frequently pardoned, as they were throughout the century (but less so after his *Enquiry*), then the deterrent effect is weakened because the association is impaired.[19] Logically then, if capital punishment deters strongly, then why not employ that prevention against more and more crimes? This multiplication of capital crimes is, of course, what happened over the course of the 17th and 18th centuries.

But Beccaria brings other lines of argument to bear against making punishments more horrible and severe. To understand these arguments better, we might compare his reasoning to that of William Blackstone, whose famous *Commentaries* came out almost simultaneously with Beccaria's *Essay*. Blackstone was able to justify capital punishment by reference to the Bible and "the social contract,"[20] but he was nonetheless uncomfortable with applying capital punishment to crimes only *mala prohibita* rather than *mala in se*. Blackstone could imagine capital punishment being invoked to stop loaded wagons from damaging roads, since current penalties had been unable to curtail the practice.[21] Such a law would lack proportion, Blackstone felt.

Beccaria assumes with Blackstone and virtually every other 18th century theorist that there should be a proportion between the crime and the punishment, and that the current system failed in that respect. Beccaria argues effectively that the proportional classification of crimes and punishments should be based on "the injury done to society" (27), not the crime's degree of evil, for only "the Almighty ... who cannot receive impressions of pleasure, or pain, and who alone, of all other beings, acts without being acted upon" (27) can discern gradations of evil—can, in other words, escape the subjectivity and arbitrariness that, as Locke makes clear, pervade all our judgments. Thus, physical punishment, including execution, would be possibly appropriate only when the crime involved physical injury or murder—certainly not in cases of forgery or theft.

Even for the most severe injuries to another person, however, Beccaria opposes capital punishment, and the grounds of his opposition are not solely the result of sympathy (based on the implications of Lockean perception) outweighing deterrence (based on the implications of Lockean association). Beccaria's acceptance of association and deterrence is clear enough: but he finds capital punishment inappropriate for many crimes by refining the idea of proportion. He thinks that making "the punishment as analogous as possible to the nature of the crime" would actually strengthen "this important connexion between the ideas of crime and punishment" (75). In other words, if a man commits robbery, then he should himself be "robbed," with his own goods confiscated and also (since this crime is so often "the effect of misery and despair"—read "poverty") the fruits of his forced labor taken (80).

But the power of analogy will not dispense with all capital

punishments, and Beccaria sets forth a principle that tends to soften all punishments of whatever severity. While punishment should "make the strongest and most lasting impressions on the minds of others," it should do so "with the least torment to the body of the criminal" (41–42). The logic for the important latter part of this formula is not based simply on the thesis that extreme punishments may harden the public to violence. Rather, in a seminal statement, Beccaria holds that "The certainty of a small punishment will make a stronger impression, than the fear of one more severe, if [the more severe one is] attended with the hopes of escaping" (95). If punishments are perceived to be too severe for small crimes, not only is the system reluctant to carry out the sentence, but offenders will proceed to commit a larger crime to avoid detection (95). Beccaria also makes the related argument that execution is "a terrible but momentary spectacle, and therefore a less efficacious method of deterring others, than the continued example of a man deprived of his liberty, condemned, as a beast of burden, to repair, by his labour, the injury he had done to society" (134). Only when a citizen by simply remaining alive threatens "the security of the nation" (as in revolutionary times) can the state illegally but justifiably take from him what it has no power to give, his life – and even then it is a sign of the government's weakness, Beccaria says.

Beccaria's consideration of *Crimes and Punishments* employs, as we might expect and as we have seen, a Lockean model of the mind. Some part of the power of Beccaria's amalgamation and extension of previous humanitarian sentiments must be due to the grounding of his argument in a coherent and widely accepted model of the mind. But, as I have argued, while Locke's discussion of "perception" (and the relationship of language to sensations) tends to support Beccaria's progressive, humane stance on the one hand, the implications of retention (and association) tend to call it into question on the other. As Locke writes in his discussion of "Power," "*when we compare present Pleasure or Pain with future* (which is usually the case in the most important determinations of the Will) *we often make wrong Judgments of them*" because "Objects, near our view, are apt to be thought greater, than those of a larger size, that are more remote" (275). Such psychological facts suggest that only severe punishments will function as an effective deterrent. Although Beccaria's argument against severe punishments, especially capital punishment, is appealing, and Beccaria eventually came to be seen as the most important force in the abolition of torture, the more humane treatment of criminals, and the eventual elimination of capital punishment for many laws, the psychological case on Lockean grounds for a powerful deterrent arguably fettered the movement toward reform, authorizing both the celebration (in spirit) and the disregard (in particulars) of Beccaria and his followers.

Notes

1. References to Beccaria's *Essay* will be to the anonymous translation, *An Essay on Crimes and Punishments ... with The Commentary by Voltaire* (London: E. Hodson, 1801), and will be cited in the text. The editor of the 1822 Paris edition is quoted in James Heath, *Eighteenth Century Penal Theory* (London: Oxford University Press, 1963) 110. Useful introductions to Beccaria can be found in Marcello Maestro, *Cesare Beccaria and the Origins of Penal Reform* (Philadelphia: Temple University Press, 1973), and Franco Venturi, *Settecento riformatore: Da Muratori a Beccaria* (Turin, Italy: Giulio Einaudi, 1969).

2. The quotation is from Leon Radzinowicz's massive *History of English Criminal Law*, 5 vols. (London: Stevens and Sons, 1948–86), 1: 286. For similar assessments, in addition to those works cited above, see Harry Barnes, *The Story of Punishment* (Montclair, N.J.: Patterson Smith, 1972), 95; Phillip Mackey, *Hanging in the Balance: The Anti-Capital Punishment Movement in New York State, 1776–1861* (New York: Garland, 1982), 49; David Cooper, *The Lesson of the Scaffold: The Public Execution Controversy in Victorian England* (Athens: Ohio University Press, 1974), 29; Marcello Maestro, *Voltaire and Beccaria as Reformers of Criminal Law* (Morningside Heights, N.Y.: Columbia University Press, 1942).

3. Cooper, *The Lesson of the Scaffold*, 6, 31–32; Michel Foucault, *Discipline and Punish: The Birth of the Prison* (New York: Pantheon, 1977), 9. See also L. A. Parry, *The History of Torture in England* (Montclair, N.J.: Patterson Smith, 1975).

4. Barnes, *The Story of Punishment*, 95.

5. Cooper, *The Lesson of the Scaffold*, 31–32.

6. Radzinowicz, *History of English Criminal Law*, 1: 300.

7. An exception is David Young's "Despotism and the Road to Freedom: Cesare Beccaria and Eighteenth-Century Lombardy," in *Studies*

in Eighteenth-Century Culture, vol. 13, ed. O. M. Brack, Jr. (Madison: University of Wisconsin Press, 1984), 271–79.

8. The lack of attention to Beccaria and 18th century psychology (and especially Locke) can be exemplified by noting that Locke's name does not appear in Maestro's fine book on Beccaria and the origins of penal reform, cited in note 1.

9. MacLean, *John Locke and English Literature of the Eighteenth Century* (New Haven: Yale University Press, 1936), v; Howell, *Eighteenth-Century British Logic and Rhetoric* (Princeton University Press, 1971), 277.

10. See Irving Louis Horowitz, *Claude Helvetius: Philosopher of Democracy and Enlightenment* (New York: Paine-Whitman, 1954), 144–145; see also John Randall, *Making of the Modern Mind* (New York: Houghton Mifflin, 1940), 316–317.

11. While the centrality of these strategies has not been noted by Locke's readers, they are part of the tradition of "constructive scepticism" that R. S. Woolhouse, for one, sees Locke inhabiting, in *Locke* (Brighton, Sussex, England: Harvester Press, 1983), 10–14. These strategies are also common in 18th century theoretical investigations: see, for example, Condillac's *Traite des sensations,* which focuses on a speechless statue that is brought to life one sense at a time, in Georges le Roy, ed. *Oeuvres philosophiques de Condillac,* 3 vols. (Paris: Presses Universitaires de France 1947–51).

12. John Locke, *An Essay concerning Human Understanding,* ed. Peter Nidditch (Oxford: Clarendon Press, 1975), 10, 301–2, 146, 344, 451. Further references will be cited in the text, unless otherwise indicated. Locke claims to have seen "the Issue" of the cat and rat mating (451). John Yolton conveniently lists some of Locke's other cross-species, in *Locke: An Introduction* (Oxford: Basil Blackwell, 1985), 108–9.

13. Locke, *An Essay concerning Human Understanding,* 543. I have altered the punctuation after "thinks" from a comma to a semicolon. For a fascinating discussion of the soul's place and nature, see Yolton, *Thinking Matter: Materialism in Eighteenth-Century Britain* (Minneapolis: University of Minnesota Press, 1983), esp. 7, 9, 86, 99, 120, 132, 133, 138, 144, 155, 157, 163, 166, 168, 170, 175, 186, and 196. See also Hopewell Selby, "'Never Finding Full Repast': Satire and Self-Extension in the Early Eighteenth Century," in *Probability, Time, and Space in Eighteenth Century Literature,* ed. Paula Backsheider (New York: AMS, 1979), 113–139.

14. Graeme Newman, *The Punishment Response* (Philadelphia: Lippincott, 1978), 91.

15. Johnson, *The Rambler,* volumes 3, 4, and 5 of the *Yale Edition of the Works of Samuel Johnson* (New Haven: Yale University Press, 1969), 4: 242.

16. Johnson, *Sermons,* volume 14 of the *Yale Edition* (New Haven: Yale University Press, 1978), 279. For a discussion of Johnson's attitude toward capital punishment and his role in the case of William Dodd, a case that

stimulated considerable pressure toward reform, see Radzinowicz, *History of English Criminal Law*, 1: 336–38, 456–64.

17. Heath, *Eighteenth-Century Penal Theory*, 170.

18. William Paley, *The Principles of Moral and Political Philosophy*, 2 vols. (London: R. Faulder, 1804), 2: 326.

19. See Radzinowicz, *History of English Criminal Law*, 1: 135–36, 407, and 409.

20. William Blackstone, *Of Public Wrongs*, volume 4 of the *Commentaries on the Laws of England* (Boston: Beacon Press, 1962), 8–9.

21. Cited in Heath, *Eighteenth-Century Penal Theory*, 184.

Henry Fielding and "A Certain Wooden Edifice" Called the Gallows

GAYLE R. SWANSON

It is perhaps natural for us to think of 18th century England as a world of elegance and formality—one where the neoclassical reverence for order, harmony, and balance is manifest in everything from architecture to landscape gardening; a polite, urbane world of decorum and good breeding; of china vases, French brocade gowns, and silk knee breeches. We picture London, with its lavish salons and ballrooms, its theaters and coffeehouses, the tree-lined promenade in St. James Park, the fashionable shops in the Strand. We may sometimes tend to forget, in other words, those less pleasant realities that inspired Gay's *The Beggar's Opera*, for example, and his "Trivia; or, the Art of Walking the Streets of London," and the even grimmer scenes of Hogarth's "Gin Lane," "The Cock Pit," and "The Reward of Cruelty," of Smollett's *Roderick Random* and Fielding's *Jonathan Wild*—the turbulent London underworld of poverty, alcoholism, gambling, and prostitution; of pickpockets, thieves, and organized street gangs; of violent crime so rampant that it intruded into the everyday lives of such citizens as Horace Walpole, who was almost killed by a robber's bullet and who declared in 1752 that in the city of London, "one is forced to travel, even at noon, as if one was going to battle."[1]

Describing the conditions in the early 1730s, Tobias Smollett had written:

> England was at this period infested with robbers, assassins, and incendiaries, the natural consequence of degeneracy, corruption, and the want of police in the interior government of the kingdom. This defect in great measure, arose from an absurd notion, that laws necessary to prevent those acts of cruelty, violence and

> rapine, would be incompatible with the liberty of the British subjects.... Thieves and robbers were now become more desperate and savage than ever they had appeared since mankind was civilized. ... they wounded, maimed, and even murdered ... through a wantonness of barbarity.[2]

With this suggestion that the existence of an organized body of police would be a logical way to help prevent crime in the streets of London, Smollett was indeed taking a stand in opposition to the overwhelming majority of his fellow citizens, who staunchly believed—as the British continued to believe well into the 19th century—that a professional police force would constitute an intolerable threat to their individual freedoms.[3] Thus rejecting the notion of creating such a force to act as a deterrent to crime, the English government responded to the ever-growing lawlessness in virtually the only way it could respond: by ever widening the scope of what was called "terror," or, in other words, the threat of the death penalty.[4]

In 1700, when William of Orange was on the throne, the statutes of English criminal law contained some 50 offenses punishable by execution.[5] By 1714, when Queen Anne had died and George I became king, that number had been increased to around 67.[6] And by midcentury, during the reign of George II, the number had grown to something like 100.[7] Included among such crimes was everything from murder to rape, to the wandering about of soldiers and sailors without a pass; from pocket-picking in the amount of 12 pence or over, to marking the edges of any current coin of the kingdom; from being found in the company of gypsies,[8] to housebreaking in the amount of five shillings or over.[9]

Yet the wave of violent crime was continuing to mount. "It is with the utmost regret," declared George II in a speech to Parliament in 1753, "I observe that the horrid crimes of robbery and murder are, of late, rather increased than diminished. I am sensible that works of reformation are not to be effected at once; but everybody should contribute their best endeavours: and let me earnestly recommend it to you, to continue your serious attention to this important object."[10] Whatever specific works of reformation the king may have envisioned, he could not have had a more ardent or capable servant in that endeavor than a man whom we most commonly think of as a literary figure: the satiric playwright and comic-epic novelist Henry Fielding. Indeed, so noteworthy was his work in the area of social and criminal reform that in January of 1751 a writer for the *Monthly Review* had been moved to avow:

> The public hath been hitherto not a little obliged to Mr. Fielding for the entertainment his gayer performances have afforded it; but now this gentleman hath a different claim to our thanks, for service of a more substantial nature. If he has been heretofore admired for his wit and humour, he now merits equal applause as a great magistrate, a useful and active member and a true friend to his country. As few writers have shown so great and extensive a knowledge of mankind in general, so none ever had better opportunities for being perfectly acquainted with that class which is . . . of all others the most necessary and useful to all, yet the most neglected and despised . . . the labouring part of the people.[11]

Educated as a lawyer, Fielding was commissioned in 1748 as justice of the peace for the City of Westminster, probably the roughest part of London at that time. In 1749, the year *Tom Jones* was published, his jurisdiction was extended to the county of Middlesex, and he thus became the principal magistrate for the city of London. In that office, he acted not only as a judge in criminal cases but also ordered and made arrests, examined prisoners before their cases were heard, and often served as chief witness for the prosecution.[12] And in the vast majority of these cases, the people with whom he dealt were indeed members of the laboring class—the lowest stratum of London society, whose cultural and economic deprivation Fielding had come to understand more fully than almost anyone outside that class itself. "The sufferings of the poor," he writes, "are . . . less observed than their misdeeds":

> this is the true reason why we so often hear them mentioned with abhorrence, and so seldom with pity. But if we were to make a progress through the outskirts of this town, and look into the habitations of the poor, we should there behold such pictures of human misery as must move the compassion of every heart that deserves the name of human. . . . whole families in want of every necessary of life. . . . They starve, and freeze, and rot among themselves; but they beg, and steal, and rob among their betters. There is not a parish in the Liberty of Westminster which doth not raise

thousands annually for the poor, and there is not a street in that Liberty which doth not swarm all day with beggars, and all night with thieves.... I omit to speak of the most open and violent insults which are every day committed on His Majesty's subjects in the streets and highways. They are enough known and .... grown to the most deplorable height.[13]

Fully sympathetic to the plight of London's poor, and fully aware of their role in the rising tide of lawlessness, Fielding also knew that the threat of execution that these people faced if they were ever apprehended or convicted of their crimes was not altogether an empty one. In 1749, for example, in only the city of London and the county of Middlesex, which was the northwest section of that city, out of 61 persons convicted of capital crimes, 44 were hanged. In 1750, again in London and Middlesex alone, out of 84 persons convicted, 56 were hanged.[14]

Clearly, Fielding took no pleasure in these facts. As he urged in 1751: "common humanity exacts our concern on this occasion; for that many cart-loads of our fellow-creatures are once in six weeks carried to slaughter is a dreadful consideration; and this is greatly heightened by reflecting, that, with proper care and proper regulations, much the greater part of these wretches might have been made not only happy in themselves, but very useful members of society, which they now so greatly dishonour."[15] But if Fielding was convinced that "proper care" and "proper regulations" would greatly help to deter London's lower classes from crime – and he did indeed devote a large part of his energies both as a writer and as a magistrate to securing these reforms – he was, as a student of human nature and as a criminal judge, equally convinced of the value of the death penalty in this regard. "To speak out fairly and honestly," he wrote, "though mercy may appear more amiable in a magistrate, severity is a more wholesome virtue; nay, severity to an individual may, perhaps, be in the end the greatest mercy, not only to the public in general ... but to many individuals":

> To consider a human being in the dread of a sudden and violent death: to consider that his life or death depend on your will; to reject the arguments which a good mind will officiously advance to itself; that violent temptations, necessity, youth, inadvertency,

have hurried him to the commission of a crime which hath been attended with no inhumanity; to resist the importunities . . . of a tender wife and affectionate children, who, though innocent, are to be reduced to misery and ruin by a strict adherence to justice: — these altogether form an object which whoever can look upon without emotion must have a very bad mind; and whoever, by the force of reason, can conquer that emotion, must have a very strong one.

"And what," continued Fielding, "can reason suggest on this occasion? . . . That by saving this individual I shall bring many others into the same dreadful situation":

what is the principal end of all punishment? is it not, as Lord Hale expresses it, "To deter men from the breach of laws, so that they may not offend, and so not suffer at all?" . . . No man indeed of common humanity or common sense can think the life of a man and a few shillings to be of an equal consideration, or that the law in punishing theft with death proceeds . . . with any view to vengeance. The terror of the example is the only thing proposed, and one man is sacrificed to the preservation of thousands.[16]

That the terror of the death penalty was not, in reality, functioning as a deterrent to crime, Fielding was only too well aware, however. Yet that fact in no way weakened his faith in its inherent ability to do so. Standing firm in his conviction that the gallows, or as he puts it in *Tom Jones*, "a certain wooden edifice . . . is, or at least *might be made*, of more benefit to society than almost any other public erection"[17] (italics mine), he set about to accomplish this very end: that of making capital punishment a real and practical instrument of social good, by identifying the causes of its failure as a deterrent and seeking correctives for them. And it was, in fact, only in terms of such a goal that Fielding could defend the practice of capital punishment at all: "in plain truth," he declared, "the utmost severity to offenders [will not] be justifiable unless we take every possible method of preventing the offence. . . . The subject as well as the child should be left without excuse before he is punished; for in that case alone the rod becomes the hand either of the parent or the magistrate."[18]

During the six years from his appointment as magistrate to his death in 1754, Fielding produced four important treatises on social order and the law: "A Charge to the Grand Jury" (1749), "A True State of the Case of Bosavern Penlez" (1749), "An Inquiry into the Causes of the Late Increase of Robbers, &c." (1751), and "A Proposal for Making an Effectual Provision for the Poor, &c." (1753). In addition, in 1752, he began the *Covent-Garden Journal*, a periodical that in great measure he devoted to the task of rousing the general public to their own responsibilities in crime prevention and of educating them to the conditions and practices in their society that were not merely failing to deter crime but were actually fostering it. Throughout the body of these writings Fielding deals with the deterrent effect of capital punishment by focusing on three areas of weakness in that regard: the apprehension and arrest of those who commit capital crimes, the prosecution and conviction of such criminals, and the manner in which their sentences are carried out.

Like Tobias Smollett, Fielding was astounded at the absurdity of the English people in rejecting a system of professional police and in thus giving the felon a very large part of what Fielding calls the "encouragement" with which he "flatters himself": "his hopes of escaping from being apprehended."[19] "I am afraid, gentlemen," he argued in his "Charge to the Grand Jury" in 1749, "this word liberty, though so much talked of, is but little understood. What other idea can we have of liberty than that it is the enjoyment of our lives, our persons, and our properties in security...!"[20] What then existed as a London police force was three groups of incompetent and often corrupt amateurs. First, a relatively small body of parish constables—primarily tradesmen who received no pay for their services and who generally kept well out of the way when any kind of danger threatened.[21] Second, a fairly large number of nightwatchmen, of whom Fielding says in *Amelia*:

> [They are] chosen out of those poor old decrepit people who are, from their want of bodily strength, rendered incapable of getting a livelihood by work. These men, armed only with a pole, which some of them are scarce able to lift, are to secure the persons and houses of his Majesty's subjects from the attacks of gangs of young, bold, stout, desperate, and well-armed villains. . . .
>   If the poor old fellows should run away from such enemies, no

one I think can wonder, unless it be that they were able to make their escape.[22]

And third, there was the odd assortment of private citizens known as "thief-catchers" or "thief-takers"—men who were paid a fee by the government upon the conviction of any criminal whom they had apprehended.[23]

Doing everything he could do to strengthen and reform this system, despite the popular consensus against it, Fielding even went so far as to form his own secret group of loyal and highly competent thief-takers,[24] the prototypes of modern detectives and now known as the "Bow Street Runners." The only way he could publicly support their work, however, was to defend thief-takers in general, even though he knew that the great majority of them were dishonest and treacherous[25] and that most people regarded them, as they did any kind of informer, as, in his own words, "odious and contemptible": "Nothing, I am sensible, is more vain than to encounter popular opinion with reason; nor more liable to ridicule than to oppose general contempt, and yet I will venture to say, that if to do good to society be laudable, so is the office of a thief-catcher; and if to do this good at the extreme hazard of your life be honourable, then is this office honourable."[26]

Concerning the prosecution and conviction of capital criminals and the weaknesses in this process that undermine the deterrent effect of the death penalty, Fielding presents his most extended argument in the treatise whose full title is "An Inquiry into the Causes of the Late Increase of Robbers, &c. with some Proposals for Remedying this Growing Evil, in which The Present Reigning Vices are impartially exposed; and the Laws that relate to the Provision for the Poor, and to the Punishment of Felons are largely and freely examined." Approaching his subject in terms of the great hope that felons have of avoiding the death penalty, he identifies six reasons that the public too often fails in its responsibility to cooperate in the prosecution of such criminals. After dismissing the fear of reprisal, for example, as "too absurd" and apathy as "too infamous, to be reasoned with," he concentrates on the type of citizen who is "Tender-hearted, and cannot take away the life of a man."[27] When anyone—either as a victim, or a witness, or a juryman—in any way inhibits or falsifies judicial procedure in an effort to extend mercy to capital criminals, that person is, Fielding contends, "guilty of a high offence against the public good":

> To desire to save these wolves in society may arise from benevolence, but it must be the benevolence of a child or a fool,[28] who mistakes the true objects of his passion. . . . Such tender-heartedness is indeed barbarity, and resembles the meek spirit of him who would not assist in blowing up his neighbour's house to save a whole city from the flames. . . . the life of a man [is] concerned; but of what man? . . . one . . . by whom the innocent are put in terror, affronted and alarmed with threats and execrations, endangered with loaded pistols, beat with bludgeons, and hacked with cutlasses, . . . and all this without any respect to age, or dignity, or sex. Let the good-natured man, who hath any understanding, place this picture before his eyes, and then see what figure in it will be the object of his compassion.[29]

After going on to examine in detail a number of ways in which the laws themselves hamper the effort to convict felons—explaining, for instance, how the rules of evidence are both too restrictive and too easily manipulated—Fielding then makes bold to address the practices of the king himself. The granting of royal pardons to capital criminals is, Fielding contends, yet another major hope that they have of escaping punishment and yet another reason, therefore, for the death penalty's failure as a deterrent. "If . . . the terror of this example is removed (as it certainly is by frequent pardons) the design of the law is rendered totally ineffectual," Fielding maintains; "the lives of the persons executed are thrown away, and sacrificed rather to the vengeance than to the good of the public. . . . This I am confident may be asserted, that pardons have brought many more men *to* the gallows than they have saved from it" (italics mine).[30]

The final and perhaps most singular reason for the death penalty's failure as a deterrent Fielding posits in the nature and practice of public executions themselves. One of the first and one of the few to contend that public hangings were so far from creating the example that they were actually destroying it, Fielding explains:

> The design of those who first appointed executions to be public, was to add the punishment of shame to that of death; in order to

make the example an object of greater terror. But experience has shown us that the event is directly contrary to this intention. Indeed, a competent knowledge of human nature might have foreseen the consequence. To unite the ideas of death and shame is not so easy as may be imagined; [because] all ideas of the latter [are] absorbed by the former. To prove this, I will appeal to any man who hath seen an execution, or a procession to an execution; let him tell me, when he hath beheld a poor wretch . . . just on the verge of eternity, all pale and trembling . . ., whether the idea of shame hath ever intruded on his mind? much less will the bold daring rogue, who glories in his present condition, inspire the beholder with any such sensation.[31]

Exactly what sensations are in fact inspired in the spectators by this latter type of criminal—the "daring rogue" who goes to the gallows with a sense of defiant pride and triumph—Fielding had also seen at firsthand: the event, he tells us, is "attended with the compassion of the meek and tender-hearted, and with the applause, admiration and envy, of all the bold and hardened. . . . And if he hath sense enough to temper his boldness with any degree of decency, his death is spoken of by many with honour, by most with pity, and by all with approbation."[32] Arguing, in other words, that human nature simply will not allow those who witness a hanging to react in the way that the legislature seems to believe they will, Fielding recommends that executions be not only private but immediate: "when executions are delayed so long as they sometimes are, the punishment and not the crime is considered; and no good mind can avoid compassionating a set of wretches who are put to death we know not why."[33]

Human nature is not, however, the only focus of Fielding's argument for the abolishment of public executions. It was the entire social spectacle of a hanging day that concerned him—the fact that such an occasion is held, "it almost appears, to make a holiday for, and to entertain, the mob."[34] Underscoring this point in the *Covent-Garden Journal* and seeking thereby to bring public pressure on the members of Parliament, Fielding describes in some detail the crude sports and antics of the people during an actual procession to the gallows and at the hanging itself. "I could, I think, paint the scene in a more ludicrous light if I had chose it, but I do not," he then says. "It is not my intention to raise my reader's mirth, but his indignation, and by that means to prevail with those in whose power it is, to prevent for the future the exhibiting of these horrid farces, which do really reflect so great a scandal to the nation and so much disgrace to humanity." "The real fact is," Fielding concludes, "that instead of making the gallows an object of terror, our executions contribute to make it an object of contempt in the eye of the malefactor; and we sacrifice the lives of men, not for the reformation but for the diversion of the populace."[35]

Public executions continued in England for more than another hundred years. Yet the fact remains that the body of Fielding's arguments concerning capital punishment in particular and criminal reform in general were to have a significant impact in the 18th century and beyond. As Leon Radzinowicz remarks in his seminal *History of English Criminal Law*, "Whether or not one is in agreement with Fielding's conclusions, the permanent value of his pioneer research into the origins of crime must be fully acknowledged."[36] Recognizing Fielding as a legal authority whose writings are "known to have exercised a deep influence on the moulding of public opinion," Radzinowicz gives attention to "An Inquiry into the Causes of the Late Increase of Robbers, &c." as an essay "of unique importance"[37] in this regard—"a striking record of the manifold factors which led to anti-social behaviour"[38] and "equally notable from the point of view of penal policy."[39] Both as a writer and as a magistrate, Fielding is indeed a central figure in the annals of criminal justice,[40] a man whose work itself, as M. Dorothy George affirms in *London Life in the Eighteenth Century*, "marks a turning-point in the social history of London."[41]

Notes

1. Quoted in Malvin R. Zirker, *Fielding's Social Pamphlets: A Study of "An Enquiry into the Causes of the Late Increase of Robbers" and "A Proposal for Making an Effectual Provision for the Poor,"* University of California English Studies, no. 31 (Berkeley and Los Angeles: University of California Press, 1966), 2.

2. Quoted in Leon Radzinowicz, *The Movement for Reform, 1750–1833,* vol. 1 of *A History of English Criminal Law and Its Administration from 1750* (New York: Macmillan, 1948), 28–29.

3. While fully acknowledging the fact that "According to British standards, all the countries that had police forces were despotic" (13), Patrick Pringle (*Hue and Cry: The Story of Henry and John Fielding and Their Bow Street Runners* (New York: Morrow, n.d.) suggests that in England, "The main reason for opposition to the police idea was not the love of freedom but hatred of change.... Britons were born into a world without policemen and took it for granted there would never be policemen" (15).

4. Pringle, *Hue and Cry,* 48.

5. James B. Christoph, *Capital Punishment and British Politics: The British Movement to Abolish the Death Penalty, 1945–57* (Chicago: University of Chicago Press, 1962), 14.

6. Pringle, *Hue and Cry,* 49.

7. I arrived at this figure on the basis of Radzinowicz's statement that "Thirty-three capital offences were created in George II's reign [1727–60] – about one for every year" (4). As Radzinowicz goes on to explain, however, "It would be wrong to identify the number of capital statutes with the number of cases in which capital punishment could be inflicted. ... it is necessary to bear in mind the composite character of these enactments, each of which was so broadly framed as to allow for the infliction of the death penalty for a considerable number of variations of the same offence.... The actual scope of the death penalty was therefore often as much as three or four times as extensive as the actual number of capital provisions would seem to indicate" (5).

8. Radzinowicz, *The Movement for Reform,* 10–11.

9. Ibid., 636.

10. Quoted in Radzinowicz, *The Movement for Reform,* 425, n. 1.

11. Quoted in Radzinowicz, *The Movement for Reform,* 402, n. 12.

12. Pringle, *Hue and Cry,* 42.

13. "A Proposal for Making an Effectual Provision for the Poor, &c.," *Legal Writings,* vol. 13 of *The Complete Works of Henry Fielding, Esq.,* ed. William Ernest Henley, 16 vols. (London: Cass, 1967), 141–42.

14. Radzinowicz, *The Movement for Reform,* 147.

15. "An Inquiry into the Causes of the Late Increase of Robbers, &c.," *Legal Writings,* vol. 13 of *The Complete Works of Henry Fielding, Esq.,* ed. William Ernest Henley, 16 vols. (London: Cass, 1967), 127.

16. "An Inquiry," 119–21.

17. *Tom Jones, Vol. II,* vol. 4 of *The Complete Works of Henry Fielding, Esq.,* ed. William Ernest Henley, 16 vols. (London: Cass, 1967), 54; bk. 7, ch. 15.

18. "An Inquiry," 126.

19. "An Inquiry," 98.

20. "A Charge to the Grand Jury," *Legal Writings*, vol. 13 of *The Complete Works of Henry Fielding, Esq.*, ed. William Ernest Henley, 16 vols. (London: Cass, 1967), 209.

21. F. Homes Dudden, *Henry Fielding: His Life, Works, and Times*, 2 vols. (Hamden, Conn.: Archon, 1966), 765–66.

22. *Amelia, Vol. I*, vol. 6 of *The Complete Works of Henry Fielding, Esq.*, ed. William Ernest Henley, 16 vols. (London: Cass, 1967), 16; bk. 1, ch. 2.

23. Dudden, *Henry Fielding*, 767.

24. Pringle makes the additional point that "Fielding had no authority to form a police force of even that small size. Had he done it openly he would doubtless have been condemned by the public for a breach of the Constitution" (89).

25. Pringle, *Hue and Cry*, 96.

26. "An Inquiry," 108.

27. "An Inquiry," 109.

28. Eight years before his appointment as magistrate, Fielding had made a statement against false benevolence with a similar focus in an article in the *Champion* (27 March 1740) in which he defines his favorite human quality of "good-nature" by explaining "what it is not": "to be averse to, and repine at the punishment of vice and villainy, is not the mark of good-nature but folly; on the contrary, to bring a real and great criminal to justice is, perhaps, the best natured office we can perform to society, and the prosecutor, the juryman, the judge, and the hangman himself may do their duty without injuring this character; nay, the last office, if properly employed may in truth be the best natured, as well as the highest post of honour in the kingdom" (258–59).

29. "An Inquiry," 111–12.

30. "An Inquiry," 121.

31. "An Inquiry," 122–23.

32. "An Inquiry," 122.

33. "An Inquiry," 123.

34. "An Inquiry," 123.

35. Quoted in B. M. Jones, *Henry Fielding, Novelist and Magistrate* (London: George Allen & Unwin, 1933), 205.

36. Radzinowicz, *The Movement for Reform*, 403.

37. Ibid., 401.

38. Ibid., 404.

39. Ibid., 403.

40. Fielding "founded the English police," Pringle states flatly: "Why this fact has been ignored by historians is beyond comprehension" (77). "Fielding not only introduced into England the idea of a preventive police," continues Pringle, "but he also showed England (and the world) that it was possible for a state to have an efficient police force without becoming a police state. Almost alone in his age he realized that an Englishman's

liberty did not depend on slavish worship of the English Constitution, but could be lost that way. In this he was eighty years ahead of the country as a whole" (113).

41. M. Dorothy George, *London Life in the Eighteenth Century* (New York: Harper, 1964), 6.

Crime and Punishment in 1777: The Execution of the Reverend Dr. William Dodd and Its Impact upon His Contemporaries

JOHN J. BURKE, JR.

The Reverend Dr. William Dodd died at the age of 48, in the prime of his life, after being hung by the neck at Tyburn according to the laws of England on Monday, June 27, 1777, before a crowd of more than 30,000 spectators. His execution remains one of the most famous or infamous instances of capital punishment in England during the 18th century. Men of the cloth are not commonly found among the ranks of condemned criminals. Yet William Dodd was a clergyman in England's established church, an ordained Anglican priest, and a preacher of considerable talent and fame. Moreover, his life was taken for something that would not be a capital offense today. The crime for which he lost his life was forgery. He had signed the name of his one-time patron on a bond for 4,200 pounds. The fraud was detected almost immediately. He was then arrested, charged, and brought to trial. He was convicted of forgery on February 22, 1777, but a legal technicality held up the final verdict until May 26, 1777, when he was sentenced to be hung by the neck until dead. Dodd's case is especially instructive because it involved some of his century's most famous names. He was hoping to save his life with an appeal for clemency, and he turned to Samuel Johnson for help. Johnson responded affirmatively to Dodd's plea. His efforts on Dodd's behalf in 1777 would later receive close attention in the *Life of Johnson* published by Hawkins in 1787 as well as in the more famous *Life* published by Boswell in 1791. The differences in the accounts by Hawkins and Boswell are striking, even startling, and they reveal much about the range of attitudes toward capital punishment in late 18th century England.[1]

Capital punishment touches upon basic human values because it involves issues of justice, the character of authority, the nature of government, and, perhaps most importantly, our respect for human life. Johnson had grappled with some of these issues long before the Reverend William Dodd's trial in 1777. *Rambler* 114 is one conspicuous instance.[2] It was originally published on April 20, 1751, and it remains the most complete statement of Johnson's considered views on capital punishment. It is not his only statement because what he says there is echoed in other places, most notably at the beginning of Sermon 26 on the duties of governors and in the final paragraph of *Adventurer* 50 whose chief subject is quite another matter.[3] All of these make it obvious that Johnson was deeply concerned about capital punishment and the uses to which it had been put. He begins *Rambler* 114 by drawing attention to the irrationality of sentencing in the English courts. "A slight perusal of the laws by which the measures of vindictive and coercive justice are established will discover so many disproportions between crimes and punishments, such capricious distinctions of guilt, and such confusions of remissness and severity, as can scarcely be believed to have been produced by public wisdom sincerely and calmly studious of public happiness" (242). Nor is there much room for faith in the social value of capital punishment. The rising rate of crime, if anything, seemed to him to contradict customary confidence in the value of capital punishment as a deterrent (243).

Johnson does not argue for the elimination of the death penalty in *Rambler* 114, as Beccaria would in 1764, but he does recommend that it be sharply restricted, and he offers philosophic, social, and legal reasons to support that view.[4] He argues that restrictions on the use of capital punishment would bring about more reasonable relationships between the crimes committed and the penalties imposed, and that would in turn bring about an improvement in the system of justice. The situation at the time he was writing was one where good citizens often refused to cooperate with authorities during criminal investigations. Johnson believed they were reacting to the evident absurdities in the administration of justice, and so were unwilling to believe that "to pick the pocket and to pierce the heart is equally criminal." If the death penalty were to be limited only to the most serious crimes, he thought more people would be willing to cooperate with the authorities: "All laws against wickedness are ineffectual unless some will inform, and some will prosecute; but till we mitigate the penalties for mere viola-tions of property, information will always be hated, and prosecution dreaded. The heart of a good man cannot but recoil at the thought of punishing a slight injury with death; especially when he remembers that the thief might have procured safety by another crime, from which he was restrained only by his remaining virtue" (246).

The views expressed in *Rambler* 114 were to be put to the test 27 years later when Johnson became involved in the public events of the Dodd affair. It may be worth reviewing at this point the events that led to the Reverend Dr. William Dodd being charged with the crime of forgery.[5] Dodd came from modest circumstances, born in Lincolnshire, the eldest son of a simple vicar. As a young man he entered Clare Hall, Cambridge, as a sizar, that is, as a scholarship student, undoubtedly helped by his father's ecclesiastical connections. The young Dodd did very well at Cambridge, but moved to London shortly after receiving his degree. Apparently he thought at first he could make his way in the world as a writer, but then decided upon a career in the church, believ-ing it to be more secure. He was ordained a deacon in 1751, and a priest in 1753. Another crucial turning point in his life was his marriage to Mary Perkins, the daughter of a humble church verger, in April 1751. The newly ordained William Dodd was nothing if not ambitious, and his new wife seems to have been more than willing to aid and abet his schemes. The pattern of his activities in the 1750s and 1760s suggests that his design was to acquire fame and fortune by associating with the fashionable and the wealthy. He began to preach sermons, with great success, employing a stagey and theatrical manner. We have confirma-tion of this from Horace Walpole who accompanied Prince Edward and his party on a visit to Magdalen House on January 27, 1760, and who then reported on the visit the next day in a letter to his friend George Montagu. While deploring the general atmosphere of theater and popery, Walpole conceded that "a young clergyman, one Dodd" preached "very eloquently and touchingly."[6]

An unmistakable sign that the ambitious Dodd was willing to cross over accepted boundaries in the pursuit of self-interest occurs three years before he would be charged with forgery. Early in 1774 it became public knowledge that his wife had offered a bribe of 3,000 pounds to the wife of the lord chancellor in hopes of obtaining the living of St.

George's, Hanover Square, for her husband. In spite of the public em-
barrassment that followed upon this revelation, and the ridicule that
came with the nickname "Dr. Simony," Dodd somehow managed to
keep his hold on public favor. His ultimate undoing would come
through another of the means he had used to augment his income. In
the 1760s he took the sons of wealthy noblemen into his home and
acted as their tutor. One of the young boys he took in was Philip
Dormer Stanhope, nephew and heir to the famous fourth earl of
Chesterfield, who first came to him in 1766, at the age of ten. Seven
years later, in 1773, this same young man, now 17, following the death
of his uncle, became the fifth earl of Chesterfield. It was Dodd's connection with the fifth earl of Chesterfield, who was only 21 years of age in
1777, that was to prove fatal.

By 1777 the Reverend Dodd was experiencing serious financial
problems. His solution to his embarrassments was to forge the young
Lord Chesterfield's signature on a bond for 4,200 pounds. The immediate purpose, we are told, was to get his hands on 300 pounds to
pay off pressing debts.[7] Given the previous connection between the
two, and Dodd's status as a clergyman in the Church of England, it was
not expected that charges would be pressed, especially since he had
made every effort to make full restitution once the forgery was un-
covered. However, charges were pressed, and the Reverend Dr. Dodd
found himself on trial for forgery and not long after convicted of a
felony that carried with it the death penalty.

The amount of the forged bond has a bearing on Dodd's troubles.
If we follow the practice of multiplying by 50 in order to come up with
a sum that makes sense in our own times, we find that the young earl
would have been answerable for the equivalent of a quarter of a million
dollars in our money. Not even a wealthy English earl could afford to
be blasé about that amount. Moreover, forgery would have been considered a serious crime no matter what the circumstances. Forgery
represented a threat to the legal underpinnings of society where so
much value is located in the guarantee provided by a signature. When
we combine the nature of the crime with the amount of money involved,
we get a better sense of why Dodd's actions were taken so seriously.

When we take our measure of Johnson's response to Dodd's misfor-
tunes, we should recognize that he did not feel much sympathy for

Dodd.[8] This criminal was not a victim of circumstances. Dodd was, in fact, well off, or should have been. By 1777 his annual income was at least 800 pounds. He possessed the income from at least two livings and a prebendary, as well as income from his chapels.[9] If he was a victim at all, he was a victim of his own vanity and greed. He had lived a flamboyant life-style, one that had early on earned him the sobriquet "the macaroni parson." His life-style was objectionable not just because he was living so far beyond his means, but because he was a clergyman living so far beyond his means. There was also an odor of treachery in his actions. When he forged the bond, he was betraying whatever trust there had been between himself and his young patron. Moreover, this patron had according to all reports treated his tutor with unfailing kindness. That kindness included the grant in 1774 of a living at Winge in Buckinghamshire, and that at the time when Dodd was in deep disgrace over the attempted bribe of Lady Apsley. The Reverend Dr. Dodd would never be celebrated for his gratitude.

We owe our inherited understanding of how Samuel Johnson conducted himself during the Dodd case primarily to the account we find in Boswell's *Life of Johnson*. Boswell provides us with a deft summary of the events that led up to Dodd's plea for Johnson's help:

> And here [in the year 1777] is the proper place to give an account of Johnson's humane and zealous interference in behalf of the Reverend Dr. William Dodd, formerly Prebendary of Brecon, and chaplain in ordinary to his Majesty; celebrated as a very popular preacher, an encourager of charitable institutions, and authour of a variety of works, chiefly theological. Having unhappily contracted expensive habits of living, partly occasioned by licentiousness of manners, he in an evil hour, when pressed by want of money, and dreading an exposure of his circumstances, forged a bond of which he attempted to avail himself to support his credit, flattering himself with hopes that he might be able to repay its amount without being detected. The person, whose name he thus rashly and criminally presumed to falsify, was the Earl of Chesterfield, to whom he had been tutor, and who, he perhaps, in the warmth of his feelings, flattered himself would have generously paid the money in case of an alarm being taken, rather than suffer him to fall a victim to the dreadful consequences of violating the law against forgery, the most dangerous crime in a commercial country; but the unfortunate divine had the mortification to find

that he was mistaken. His noble pupil appeared against him, and he was capitally convicted.[10]

The importance of the Dodd affair to Boswell is that it is so clearly an instance of "Johnson's humane and zealous interference" in behalf of someone in distress. It is for him a vivid illustration of Johnson's general humanity and thus a forceful refutation of Mrs. Thrale's charge that Johnson however charitable was not a really active friend, and would not in fact so much as lift a finger in someone's behalf.[11] Johnson's willingness to help in this case is all the more remarkable because it involved someone whom he did not really like or approve of. It is clear from what he says in a letter to Boswell describing his dismay over Dodd's execution that he was never under any illusion about the man he was trying to help: "[Dodd's] moral character is very bad: I hope all is not true that is charged upon him."[12] Another letter, this one to his close friend the Reverend Dr. John Taylor, dated May 19, 1777, shows a similar coolness toward Dodd personally, and confirms what we are told in Boswell:

> Poor Dod[d] was sentenced last week. It is a thing almost without example for a Clergyman of his rank to stand at the bar for a capital breach of morality. I am afraid he will suffer. The Clergy seem not to be his friends. The populace that was extremely clamorous against him, begin to pity him. The time that was gained by an objection, which was never considered as having any force, was of great use, as it allowed the publick resentment to cool. To spare his life, and his life is all that ought to be spared, would be now rather popular than offensive. How little he thought six months ago of being what he now is.[13]

When Johnson set out to save Dodd's life, he was acting on a conviction based on principle. That principle, it seems to me, was his opposition to capital punishment for crimes against property, the very same principle he had laid out 26 years earlier in *Rambler* 114. The importance of that principle would help explain why Johnson never made any effort to meet with Dodd. All communication between them was through intermediaries or by way of the written word. It is also clear that Johnson was not acting on his own initiative. The initiative seems to have come from Dodd, who apparently appreciated Johnson's expressive powers and saw his reputation for integrity and probity as a valuable asset in the public relations battle he was then waging. Dodd seems to have asked the countess of Harrington to act as an intermediary.[14] She then wrote a letter to Johnson, delivered by Edmund Allen, asking him to do what he could for the unfortunate Dodd. Johnson promptly replied that he would do whatever he could.

It was not easy for Johnson's biographers to determine the full extent of Johnson's activities on behalf of Dodd because of the shroud of secrecy that was cast over his actions. He took part in the campaign that gathered 23,000 signatures on a petition asking for clemency. He also wrote private letters on Dodd's behalf. What Johnson could do best was write, and so he also offered Dodd his pen. We can be virtually certain that under the circumstances Dodd was emotionally distraught and intellectually distracted, and ever so glad to have Johnson's help. It was Johnson who wrote his speech to the recorder of London, which he delivered on the day he was sentenced. It was Johnson who composed the petitions to the king and to the queen pleading for mercy. And it was Johnson who, most famous of all, composed "A Convict's Address to His Unhappy Brethren," the condemned sermon delivered by Dodd at Newgate the day before he died.[15] Since these works were passed off as Dodd's own, Johnson felt obligated to keep his role in them secret. He did admit to his friends that he had given Dodd help, but he was vague about the details of the help.[16] So in response to a query from Boswell who had seen a quote urging clemency for Dodd attributed to him in the *Public Advertiser*, Johnson replied: "The saying that was given me in the papers I never spoke; but I wrote many of his petitions, and some of his letters. He applied to me very often."[17]

All of Johnson's efforts were to come to naught. The petitions for clemency were denied, and the death sentence against Dodd was carried out. The motive behind that inflexibility can undoubtedly be traced to the sentiment expressed in Lecture 10 of the Second Part of Sir Robert Chambers's *Lectures on the English Law*, delivered at Oxford not long before Dodd's trial and execution.[18] The danger to commercial society was simply too great, and it was too widely believed that only the fear of death would deter crimes of forgery and counterfeiting.

There was also a question of precedent. The previous year David and Robert Perreau, twin brothers, had been caught in a scheme to acquire large amounts of money by forging the name of William Adair on bonds and promissory notes. Margaret Caroline Rudd, who had been passing herself off as the wife of Daniel Perreau, and herself a party to the forgery, turned in state's evidence. As a result of her testimony the two brothers were convicted of forgery and sentenced to be hung by the neck until dead. There were numerous petitions for clemency, including one presented to the queen by Robert's wife, "dressed in deep mourning" and "accompanied by her three children."[19] Moreover, the brothers continued to maintain their innocence to the very end, claiming they had been dupes of the wiles of one Margaret Caroline Rudd. Nevertheless, the petitions for clemency were denied, and the two Perreaus were executed on January 17, 1776. There was not much to justify making an exception for Dodd hardly more than a year later.

Johnson was deeply affected by Dodd's execution. The letters he wrote at the time indicate he was perhaps more pained with the intransigence of the system than moved by any philosophical opposition to capital punishment. The English legal system gives the chief executive the power to pardon or commute a sentence, or to assign a lighter one. King George III could have commuted Dodd's sentence to one of transportation. Johnson, a Tory, seems angry at the king for refusing to use his powers, and especially indignant that he refused to use them after receiving a petition on Dodd's behalf with 23,000 names on it. Yet Johnson's response ultimately became one of philosophical resignation. His attitude might be summed up best in an incident reported by Boswell under the entry for April 18, 1783, almost six years after Dodd's execution. Someone asked Johnson for an appropriate motto that might be placed under a portrait of Dodd. His reply was *currat lex*, let the law run its course. Johnson had been truly saddened by Dodd's execution, but he kept his faith in the English legal system. He was willing enough to have Dodd pardoned, but once he was hanged, he did not wish him to be made into a saint.[20]

Boswell's reaction to Dodd's execution was virtually the same as Johnson's, however much they may have differed in other matters. It is clear that he doubted the deterrent value of capital punishment and that he favored mercy for Dodd. As he put it in a letter to Johnson, dated June 9, 1777, when there was still hope that King George might grant the Reverend Dr. Dodd clemency:

> I own I am very desirous that the royal prerogative of remission of punishment should be employed to exhibit an illustrious instance of the regard which GOD's VICEREGENT will ever shew to piety and virtue. If for ten righteous men the ALMIGHTY would have spared Sodom, shall not a thousand acts of goodness done by Dr. Dodd counterbalance one crime? Such an instance would do more to encourage goodness, than his execution would do to deter from vice. I am not afraid of any bad consequence to society; for who will persevere for a long course of years in a distinguished discharge of religious duties, with a view to commit a forgery with impunity? (3: 119).

It is clear from his journals that though Boswell was in Edinburgh in the spring and summer of 1777 and therefore far removed from the daily scenes involving Dodd, he was still deeply affected by the events that led to Dodd's execution. On Friday, June 27, 1777, the day Dodd was hung at Tyburn, we find the following entry in his journal: "Looked [at] watch, thinking always of Dr. Dodd. It seemed nothing when over, in comparison of 'horrible imagining.' Yet I hoped perhaps rescue."[21] When the news reached him on July 1 that Dodd had in fact been executed, Boswell recorded his reaction as "shocked," and, devout Tory though he was, as "angry against King" for failing to use his prerogative to commute the death sentence into one of lesser punishment.[22] So disordered did he become that according to his journal he was unable to function normally for days after hearing the news of Dodd's death.

The difference between Boswell's reaction and Johnson's seems to be one of degree. Though Johnson actively opposed the death penalty for Dodd, once due process had run its course and the execution became fact there is a tone of philosophical resignation. Boswell's reaction is more personal, more emotional, more hurt. Part of this was probably rooted in his own fear of death, the same psychological phenomenon that would explain his morbid lifelong attraction to public executions.[23] It may also be worth pointing out that Dodd's was not the first case in which Boswell had to confront the issue of capital punishment for crimes against property. Only three years earlier, in

1774, he had been deeply involved in the defense of John Reid, a sheep-stealer, where capital punishment had loomed large. At the first trial Boswell succeeded in winning an acquittal for Reid, but after a second trial on a new charge of sheep-stealing, Reid was convicted and the death penalty was imposed. Boswell appealed Reid's sentence to the king, asking that the death penalty be commuted to one of transportation. The king, however, denied the petition, and John Reid was hung, insisting to the last that he was an innocent man.[24] The loss of his client, someone he had come to know and even to have some fondness for, deeply affected Boswell. Once again he fell into a deep gloom after the execution.

For another view of the events leading up to the execution of the Reverend Dr. William Dodd, we can turn to the pages of Sir John Hawkins's *Life of Johnson*, published in 1787, a little more than four years before Boswell would publish his own more famous biography of Johnson.[25] Hawkins has some serious shortcomings as a biographer, but his *Life* does provide a telling contrast with the picture that we get from Johnson's letters and Boswell's *Life*. Neither Johnson nor Boswell had known Dodd personally, though both had been in his company on one occasion. Hawkins, on the other hand, had some personal knowledge of Dodd, and that allowed him to pass on information that is not to be found in Johnson or in Boswell. Hawkins, is clearly familiar, for instance, with the places where Dodd had lived and with how he earned additional income supervising and tutoring young gentlemen in his house. The most startling information he has to offer came from the brother of Dodd's wife, a man known to Sir John because he had for a while been one of his tenants. According to his brother-in-law, the Reverend Dodd was a tireless campaigner for preferment, that is, for higher and better paying posts. His brother-in-law knew that because he himself had on occasion served as the intermediary (435). He also knew, though we are not told from what source, that Dodd "kept, in a back lane near him, a girl who went by the name of Kennedy" (435). This information gives some substance to what is only hinted at in vague language that refers to Dodd's "licentiousness of manners" or his "very bad" moral character. It tells us how far this clergyman had accommodated himself to the ways of the world. It may also be telling us why he constantly needed more money.

Hawkins will go on to present more damaging information yet, but it comes from what was already part of the public record. He reminds us, for instance, that Dodd "had rendered himself scandalous, by an offer, of money, of the first law-officer in the kingdom, of a large sum of money, for a presentation to a valuable rectory" (520). Boswell, by way of contrast, does not mention the attempted bribe, though we can be certain that he knew about it. Later Hawkins tells us that he had learned from Johnson himself that shortly before the scheduled date of execution Dodd's wife and friends offered the keeper of Newgate a bribe of one thousand pounds if he would let Dodd escape, and how when that failed on the night before his death "a number of them, with bank-notes in their pockets to the amount of five hundred pounds" looked for "an opportunity of corrupting the turnkey" (529). This same information can be found in Boswell as part of a scene in Derby where Johnson talks with the Butter family about Dodd (3: 162–63). However, this is not part of the section where Boswell describes Johnson's efforts in behalf of Dodd. As a result, it does not detract from the rhetorical emphasis on Johnson's "humane and zealous interference" on Dodd's behalf.

The purpose of Sir John Hawkins's account is clear enough. All the information he reports is damaging. His purpose clearly is to discredit William Dodd because he does not want us to sympathize with him. He does not want us to sympathize with Dodd because Hawkins, unlike Johnson, fully supported the death penalty for forgery and for other crimes against property. Justice was served for Hawkins when Dodd was hung by the neck until dead.[26] Consequently, Hawkins's account of Johnson's efforts in behalf of Dodd in his *Life* has a very different function from the one it has in Boswell's *Life*. For Hawkins, Johnson's efforts in behalf of Dr. Dodd were regrettable. They were just another example of a tendency to be soft on criminals because, as he puts it, "we live in an age in which humanity is the fashion" (521). That kind of sentimentality, in Hawkins's view, only encouraged more criminal behavior, and society becomes the ultimate victim of such misguided humanitarian actions as those in behalf of Dodd. Sir John, as a former magistrate, was convinced that in the English system of justice the accused were treated with every respect for their rights, and that English men and women had every reason to be confident in the outcomes of their system of justice. The problem in their system of justice was not that innocent human beings were executed, but that too many of the guilty were able to evade justice due to legal technicalities. Nevertheless, because there was wisdom in tempering justice with mercy, Hawkins supported the right of all convicted of capital crimes to appeal to their monarch for clemency, which Hawkins says "his majesty is ever ready to exert, in favour of those who have the least claim to it" (521). What he is saying, of course, between the lines is that Dodd did not have even the least claim to clemency.

Hawkins did not approve of Johnson's actions in the Dodd case because he did not believe that Dodd was worthy of them. But the dark uncharitable cast in Hawkins's account goes beyond the insinuation of poor judgment on Johnson's part to the further insinuation that Johnson was actually playing the part of a hypocrite. Johnson was in his actions, Hawkins tells us, guilty of a serious "inconsistency": "He assisted in the solicitations for [Dodd's] pardon, yet, in his private judgment, he thought him unworthy of it, having been known to say, that had he been the adviser of the king, he should have told him that, in pardoning Dodd, his justice in remitting the Perreaus to their sentence would have been called in question" (530). Hawkins leaves Johnson then playing a part, and playing that part without any real convictions.

But the inconsistency that Hawkins believes he has found may not be as serious as he thinks; in fact, it may not even be an inconsistency at all. It is perfectly clear when examining the record that Johnson did not do what he did because of any personal sympathy for William Dodd or from any notion of his worthiness. He did what he did as a matter of reasoned principle, because he was opposed to capital punishment for crimes against property. If as an adviser to the king he had told the king that his justice would have come into question if he commuted Dodd's sentence because the year before he had refused to grant clemency to the Perreau brothers, he would have been correct. The king's justice almost certainly would have been called into question. But not the king's mercy, and that was probably more important to Johnson. Moreover, Hawkins's language seems to assume that Johnson approved of the execution of the Perreau brothers in the previous year. That is not out of the realm of possibility, but it is not probable. I do not know of any place where Johnson made known his views about the execution of the Perreau brothers, but it is not likely that he would have approved of capital punishment in their case, either. Such a position would not be consistent with the Johnson we know from *Rambler* 114, nor with the Johnson we see operating in the Dodd case.

The case of the Reverend Dr. Dodd is a fable with many stories to tell. If I had to guess at public reaction in our own time to a sentence of death for having forged a signature on a bond, my guess is the reaction would be outrage and horror even among those who support the death penalty most strongly. It is not necessary to make a saint out of Dodd to see that taking his life was wrong.[27] Whatever Dodd's imperfections and human failings, they could hardly have been any worse than those in people who prospered and thrived because they were never caught, or if caught never convicted. Sir Robert Walpole was no saint when it came to money, and no serious effort was ever made to hang him. But to talk in such terms might be said to be unhistorical, an act that confuses our age with theirs, to judge by our standards, not theirs.

So perhaps our most lasting memories of the Dodd case may be the reactions of his contemporaries. From a modern point of view it is a moment of high honor for Samuel Johnson, and it explains his continued hold on the admiration of later generations. It also reflects well on Boswell, though not to the same degree that it does on Johnson. Boswell, being in Edinburgh when most of the events leading up to the execution of Dodd were taking place, was necessarily distant from the action. Nevertheless, it is clear he is repelled by the brutality of capital punishment and that his basic instincts were on the side of decency. I believe we see ourselves in Johnson and Boswell, but when we come upon Sir John Hawkins we see the gap between ourselves and "them" and experience the true meaning of historicism, whether new or old. For if when reading Hawkins's *Life of Samuel Johnson*, we find ourselves appalled by his approval of capital punishment, even for crimes against property, or upset at his hard-hearted disdain for the "unfortunate" Reverend Dr. Dodd, or just unsettled and possibly even angry at his debunking portrait of Johnson, then we are being given a chance to understand our own values more clearly. If that happens, then Sir John Hawkins performs a very real service for us who live in the late 20th century, and perhaps he has not outlived his usefulness after all.

Notes

1. For a broad historical account of the use of capital punishment during this period, see Leon Radzinowicz, *The Movement for Reform*, vol. 1 (1948) of *A History of English Criminal Law and Its Administration from 1750*, 5 vols. (London: Stevens, 1948–86), 1: 1–79, 83–227. See also J. M. Beattie, *Crime and the Courts in England, 1660–1800* (Princeton: Princeton University Press, 1986), especially 513–19, 530–38, 582–92.

2. *The Rambler*, ed. W. J. Bate and Albrecht Strauss, vols. 3–5 (1969) in *The Yale Edition of the Works of Samuel Johnson* (1958–), 4: 241–47. All references to *Rambler* 114 will be to this edition and after this will be included in the text. It is on the basis of *Rambler* 114 that Sir Leon Radzinowicz assigns Johnson a key role in the gradual reform of criminal law and the greater restraint in the use of capital punishment (*The Movement for Reform*, 1: 336–39).

3. *Sermons*, ed. Jean H. Hagstrum and James Gray, vol. 14 (1978) in *The Yale Edition of the Works of Samuel Johnson* (1958–), 14: 278–81. *The Idler* and *The Adventurer*, ed. W. J. Bate, John M. Bullitt, and L. F. Powell, vol. 2 (1963) of *The Yale Edition of the Works of Samuel Johnson* (1958–), 2: 366.

4. Johnson's views on capital punishment as stated in *Rambler* 114 and echoed in *Adventurer* 50 and Sermon 26 make the harsh views of Lecture 10 in Part II of the Vinerian Law Lectures even more of a mystery. There it is argued that capital punishment is necessary to prevent crimes against property, including forgery. "The experience of mankind has perhaps discovered that no punishments less than capital are sufficient for the protection of property, in which is included all the peace of society and all the tranquility of domestic life; for he that were condemned to perpetual vigilance for defence of what he now has, could never be at leisure to make his little more, or, if he had already enough, to distribute or enjoy it" (Sir Robert Chambers [in association with Samuel Johnson], *A Course of Lectures on the English Law*, 2 vols., ed. Thomas M. Curley [Madison: University of Wisconsin Press, 1986], 1: 415; see 56–59 for Curley's own comments on this matter).

5. There are a number of sources that are valuable for information about Dodd. The chief resources are the contemporary accounts of events to be found in the *Gentleman's Magazine*. Of course, James Boswell and Sir John Hawkins supply valuable information, as will be duly noted. In the 19th century Percy Fitzgerald summarized and dramatized much of what we know in *A Famous Forgery: Being the Story of "The Unfortunate" Doctor Dodd* (London: Chapman and Hall, 1865).

6. *Horace Walpole's Correspondence with George Montagu*, ed. W. S. Lewis and Ralph S. Brown, Jr., vol. 9 (1941) of *The Yale Edition of Horace Walpole's Correspondence*, 48 vols. (1937–83), 9: 273–74.

7. There has never been a satisfactory explanation of why the Reverend Dr. Dodd forged a bond for so enormous a sum as 4,200 pounds. It was reported in the February issue of the *Gentleman's Magazine* that he really only needed a small amount of the money (£300) to settle his pressing debts (GM, 47 [1777], 92–93). This claim was greeted with justifiable skepticism in a letter to the magazine printed in the following month's issue (GM, 47 [1777], 115–16). Dodd's lavish life-style was one explanation for why he needed more money, and there are hints that his financial embarrassments well exceeded the rather modest sum of 300 pounds. Another explanation involves yet another one of his money-making schemes. It was reported in the *Whitehall Evening Post* that he had been preparing a new and expensive edition of Shakespeare. Naturally there would have been a need for a large outlay of capital at the beginning of such a project, before taking subscriptions. A correspondent under the name of *Verus*, most likely a friend of Dodd's, wrote to confirm that report. The new edition of Shakespeare was also supposed to explain why Dodd had gone to Paris in 1774. He was there, we are told, to consult with the artists who were to do the engravings for the new edition (GM, 47 [1777], 172).

8. Percy Fitzgerald felt that the whole Dodd affair served to increase our admiration for Johnson, and that Johnson's lack of respect for the man he went out of his way to help was a major factor in that admiration (see *A Famous Forgery*, 130).

9. It is well to remember the incomes that other people were living on when noting that Dodd's annual income was 800 pounds a year or more. Boswell, when he first arrived in London in his early twenties, was expected to take care of all his needs—and that included playing the part of a young Scottish aristocrat—on an annual allowance of 200 pounds. Johnson supported his household—a household that included, besides himself, Anna Williams, Frank Barber, Robert Levett, Elizabeth Desmoulins and her daughter, and on some occasions Poll Carmichael—on a government pension of 300 pounds, plus whatever else he was able to add to that income with his pen.

10. *Boswell's Life of Johnson*, ed. G.B. Hill and L.F. Powell, 6 vols. (Oxford: Clarendon Press, 1934–64), 3: 139–40. All further references to Boswell's *Life of Johnson* will be to this edition and will be included in the text.

11. "As Johnson was the firmest of believers without being credulous, so he was the most charitable of mortals without being what we call an active friend. Admirable at giving counsel, no man saw his way so clearly; but he would not stir a finger for the assistance of those to whom he was willing enough to give advice: besides that, he had principles of laziness, and could be indolent by rule" (Hesther Lynch Piozzi, *Anecdotes of Dr. Johnson*, along with William Shaw, *Memoirs of Dr. Johnson*, ed. Arthur Sherbo [New York: Oxford University Press, 1974], 125). It may be of more

than passing interest that for all Mrs. Thrale's vaunted intimacy with Johnson there are virtually no references to Dodd, either in her published *Anecdotes* or in her private diaries. The sole mention of Dodd refers to the suspicion that Johnson had secretly authored his condemned sermon for him (see *Anecdotes*, 77; *Thraliana*, ed. Katharine Balderston, 2 vols. [Oxford: Clarendon, 1942], 1: 162).

12. *Letters*, ed. R. W. Chapman, 3 vols. (Oxford: Clarendon Press, 1952), No. 524, 2: 180.

13. *Letters*, No. 519, 2: 174.

14. Hawkins appears to be in error in maintaining that it was a direct appeal by Mary Dodd that won Johnson over to her husband's cause. The appeal seems to have been indirect, and it came from Lady Harrington. Boswell's account of how Johnson became involved in the Dodd affair receives independent confirmation from Johnson himself, in a letter Boswell never saw, a letter Johnson wrote to the countess of Harrington on June 25, 1777, two days before Dodd was executed. This letter along with other pertinent documents can be found in *Papers Written by Dr. Johnson and Dr. Dodd 1777, Printed from the Originals in the Possession of A. Edward Newton*, ed. R. W. Chapman (Oxford: Clarendon Press, 1926), 28–29. See also *Letters*, No. 522.1, 2: 178–79. There is still, however, a gap between fact and explanation. As far as I can determine, no one has been able to explain why the appeal for Johnson's help came through Lady Harrington. The information we do have seems to imply some kind of connection between the two in the past, and one that made Johnson especially eager to respond to a request from her.

Edmund Allen was almost certainly the key player in these events. According to Boswell, Allen, who seems to have been a friend of the countess, delivered Lady Harrington's letter into Johnson's hands. Allen had been Johnson's landlord and neighbor when he lived at Bolt Court, and he had been a fervent and active supporter of Dodd (3: 141, 497). It may have been he who saw that Johnson was the one who could do the most good for Dodd. Nevertheless, it seems highly unlikely that an approach would have been made to Johnson without Dodd's full approval, even if it was not at his initiative.

15. For an excellent discussion of Johnson's complex rhetorical strategy in the sermon he wrote for the Reverend Dr. Dodd, see Paul K. Alkon, "Johnson's Condemned Sermon," *The Unknown Samuel Johnson*, ed. John J. Burke, Jr., and Donald Kay (Madison: University of Wisconsin Press, 1983), 113–30.

16. "Though Boswell did not turn up everything, he was much more successful than Hawkins in discovering what Johnson had written during the course of the attempt to obtain a pardon for Dr. Dodd. His list, if we count Johnson's letters to Dodd, numbers fifteen items, whereas Hawkins's numbers only four" (Bertram H. Davis, *Johnson Before Boswell: A Study of Sir*

John Hawkins' "Life of Samuel Johnson" (New Haven: Yale University Press, 1960), 112).

17. *Letters*, No. 524, 2: 180; *Life*, ed. G.B. Hill and L.F. Powell, 3: 121.

18. *Lectures on the English Law*, 1: 422–23.

19. *Gentleman's Magazine*, 46 (1776), 44. For the account of the trial of the Perreau brothers, see GM, 45 (1775), 278–84; an account of their execution can be found in GM, 46 (1776), 44–45. See also James Boswell, *The Ominous Years, 1774–1776*, ed. Charles Ryskamp and Frederick A. Pottle (New York: McGraw-Hill, 1963), 353–55.

20. James Boswell, *The Applause of the Jury, 1782–1785*, ed. Irma S. Lustig and Frederick A. Pottle (New York: McGraw-Hill, 1981), 104.

21. James Boswell, *In Extremes, 1776–1778*, ed. Charles McC. Weis and Frederick A. Pottle (New York: McGraw-Hill, 1970), 131.

22. Boswell, *In Extremes*, 132.

23. See Frederick A. Pottle, *James Boswell: The Earlier Years, 1740–1776* (New York: McGraw-Hill, 1966), 18, 111–12, 354–55. See also Frank Brady, *James Boswell: The Later Years, 1769–1795* (New York: McGraw-Hill, 1984), 14, 282, 295–96.

24. Brady, *The Later Years*, 100–104.

25. Sir John Hawkins, *The Life of Samuel Johnson, LL.D.* (1787; rpt. New York: Garland, 1974). All references to Hawkins's *Life* will be to this facsimile edition, and the page numbers will be included in the text.

26. Though Hawkins opposed a grant of clemency in the case of the Reverend Dr. Dodd, he did on occasions recommend pardons while serving as a magistrate in Middlesex; see Bertram H. Davis, *A Proof of Eminence: The Life of Sir John Hawkins* (Bloomington: Indiana University Press, 1973), 199–222.

27. According to Sir Leon Radzinowicz, the movement for reform brought an end to capital punishment for Dodd's crime in the early 19th century. No one was actually executed in England for forgery after 1830, though a few individuals convicted of forgery were sentenced to death after that time; see his *History of English Criminal Law*, 1: 590–607.

The Public Execution: Urban Rhetoric and Victorian Crowds

BARRY FAULK

George Gissing's *New Grub Street* (1891) begins at the breakfast table, where an everyday domestic situation is disrupted by an unlikely subject—a hanging. With something resembling glee, the exemplar of the "new journalism," Jasper Milvain, observes to his mother and sister: "It happened to catch my eye in the paper yesterday that someone was to be hanged at Newgate this morning. There's a clear self-satisfaction in knowing that it is not oneself."[1]

Milvain's outburst and the proprieties it disrupts—its bland callousness, its self-aggrandizement—has a modern resonance. However, before our contemporary impasse regarding capital punishment, the public execution left a discernible mark on 19th century discourse in the press, Parliamentary debate, and literature. Certain features of an "urban rhetoric," tropes designed to contain the discussion of the urban execution, became recognizable. The response to public execution from such writers as Charles Dickens, William Thackeray, and George Jacob Holyoake was diverse but, in a sense, all of a piece. To detail the Victorian debate on public execution is beyond the scope of this essay; rather, I hope to contextualize the debate by tracing certain features of the discourse that centered on the gallows, or, more often than not, on the crowds gathered around the Newgate scaffold. Specifically, I will focus on Charles Dickens's and William Thackeray's interventions in the debate concerning capital punishment.

To understand the Victorian debate on public execution one needs an understanding both of the history of the scaffold and of the important role it played, not only in the history of the English penal system, but in English popular culture as well. To write the history of capital punishment in England is to write a history of festive life. The abolition of public execution in 1868 is not only a tale of the triumph of liberal sentiment, but evidence of a gradual decay of the rituals that justified certain modes of punishment. This becomes apparent when one examines the historical function of the scaffold and its relation to the "mob," and, later, to the "crowd."

The transition in England from an agrarian to a mercantile economy entailed the gradual dissolution of popular ritual forms endemic to agrarian folkways, yet certain rituals proved remarkably tenacious. Well into the 18th century one can trace the survival of what may be designated as the "urban carnivalesque."[2] The procession of those who were to be executed, a procession that traveled from Newgate Prison to Tyburn, had come to incorporate festive elements; as Bernard Mandeville scornfully observed, "All the way from Newgate to Tyburn is one continued fair, for Whores and Rogues of the meaner sort."[3] The ceremony had a leveling effect, drawing a great cross-section of society. The public execution attracted the common artisan, the wealthy thrill-seeker, and the pickpocket who simply viewed the occasion as an opportunity to practice his trade. Notable examples of the folklore that had come to be incorporated in the public execution can be seen in the crowd's repeated urge to storm the gallows to touch the deceased body, and in the popular hostility that anatomists faced when they attempted public dissections for scientific purposes.[4]

The public execution was high drama; it was punishment as "spectacle," and the parallels between execution and the theater did not go unnoticed. In *A Philosophical Enquiry into the Origin of Our Ideas of the Sublime and Beautiful* (1756), Edmund Burke contrasts the effect of the scaffold to the catharsis offered by contemporary theater and inadvertently indicates which of the two was the most popular draw: "Choose a day on which to represent the most sublime and affecting tragedy we have; appoint the most favorite actors . . . and when you have collected your audience, just at the moment when their minds are erect with expectation, let it be reported that a state criminal of high rank is on the point of being executed in the adjoining square; in a moment the emptiness of the theatre would demonstrate the comparative weakness of the imitative arts."[5]

But to acknowledge the theatrical element implicit in public execution is to leave many pertinent questions unanswered. In what way did the execution ritual function? Was there a univocal drama being played out when a criminal faced execution before the crowd? Whose interests did this drama serve? One possible interpretation can be seen in Peter Burke's assertion that public executions were a drama "carefully managed by the authorities to show the people that crime did not pay."[6] The scaffold in this view demonstrated the spectacle of sovereign power. As the French historian Robert Muchembled notes, "The view of the gallows, the smell of ashes, an encounter with an earless man spoke to all five senses of men of the time of the need to respect the established order."[7] By breaking the law, Michel Foucault observes, "the offender has touched the very person of the prince; and it is the prince ... who seizes upon the body of the condemned man and displays it marked, beaten, broken."[8] At Tyburn, then, a drama was enacted that reestablished the power of the sovereign, a power contested by the breaking of the law.

As with all good theater, the audience, in this case the crowd around the scaffold, played an essential role. The public execution appeared to concern exclusively the criminal but, as Foucault notes, "the main character was the people, whose real and immediate presence was required for the performance."[9] Dr. Johnson's words to Boswell (the latter an afficianado of public executions) come to mind: "Sir, executions are intended to draw spectators. If they do not draw spectators they don't answer their purpose."[10] If the scaffold was a dramatic exhibit of the sovereign's power over the transgressor, it was a lesson designed to be taken in by as many as possible. Spectators were needed to participate in this morality play, and even allowed festive license, as long as the underlying affirmation of the king's power was not threatened.

And, as with any good drama, the performance had effects beyond the intentions of the performers. The rituals of popular culture often inverted the intended meaning of public execution. Although the crowd sometimes vented their anger at the condemned criminal, more than likely the criminal was applauded, showered with flowers, and allowed free drinks at a tavern on the procession to Tyburn.[11] As Peter Burke observes, while "the official ritual at Tyburn expressed the attempt of the ruling classes to control ... the unofficial ritual expressed protest against these attempts."[12] Burke's point is valid, although protest is perhaps too strong a word, indicating a unified class consciousness that was not fully articulated until later in the 18th century. The success of chapbooks and broadside ballads lauding the deeds of the criminal exemplify this inversion of the execution's official meaning, illustrating how, in Muchembled's words, "the movement for the acculturation of the masses quite naturally came into conflict with popular culture, which held totally different values."[13]

The growing disparity between the official meaning of the public execution and its carnival inversion at the hands of the crowd was the despair of many noted 18th century observers. Henry Fielding's *Enquiry into the Causes of the Late Increase of Robbers* (1750) voices the typical complaint that the rogue's procession to Tyburn was "attended with the compassion of the meek and tender-hearted, and with the applause, admiration, and envy, of all the bold and hardened."[14] Not only did popular ritual diffuse the terror of the public execution but there was a mounting fear among the authorities that the leisure time allowed for executions created centers of unlawful activity.[15] It was noted with increasing alarm that executions fostered a confederacy of outcasts— vagrants, swindlers, pickpockets. Leon Radzinowicz notes that a day of public execution meant the desertion of factories and workshops in the morning and the commencement of parties in taverns and coffee shops, often centers of political dissent, on the evening before the execution.[16] By the end of the 18th century there was a growing concern that the crowd would no longer limit itself to the role of exuberant onlooker. After the French Revolution, there was the possibility of the crowd rewriting the drama being presented; the drama of the king's vengeance could become the drama of the populace's revenge.[17]

In the Victorian debate on capital punishment certain themes recur enough to become commonplace. There is a repeated insistence on the degrading nature of the "spectacle of the scaffold"; any pedagogic effect the spectacle may have for its onlookers is consistently denied. A new edge becomes apparent in what had been an already harsh rhetoric concerning the depravity of the crowd. If a noticeable shift occurs between 18th and 19th century discourse on the crowd and the scaffold, to what can it be attributed? Arguably, this transition is occasioned by a change in the perception of the crowd. Georg Lukács observes that increasingly in the 19th century the crowd is no longer understood as a disparate mass, but perceived as a Conscious Subject; after the Revolution, "the masses no longer have the appearance of a natural occurrence."[18] If the humanist reformers cast a negative verdict on the spectacle of the scaffold, such a judgment now occurs against a new backdrop—the inescapably political nature of the 19th century crowd. In this sense, lines were drawn concerning the discourse of punishment when the literary debate on capital punishment flared in the 1840s, attracting the direct intervention of writers such as Dickens and Thackeray.[19]

Dickens's ambiguous reaction to the scaffold, an entanglement of charitable sentiment and political unease, exemplifies typical tensions. As comic writer, Dickens explores the possibilities of the urban milieu and naturally responds to scenes of urban misrule. The representation of the unruly mob during the Gordon riots in *Barnaby Rudge* (1841) may be subjected to strict authorial control, yet we also have Dickens's celebrated confession to John Forster during the writing of the novel: "I have just burnt into Newgate, and am going in the next number to tear the prisoners out by the hair of their heads."[20] Dickens's realism is founded on his success at reading the metonymies of the urban crowd, and these tropes often unsettle didactic intent, or narrative control.[21] In *Oliver Twist* (1838), Fagin's hanging is set against a surreal backdrop of festive misrule, made the more grotesque by contrast with Fagin's death vigil: "Everything told of life and animation but one dark cluster of objects in the centre of all—the black stage . . . the rope and all the hideous apparatus of death."[22] The crowd's misbehavior heightens the pathos of Fagin's death; an ironic contrast is drawn between the community of thieves and the bonds tying legal society. However, although the crowd cannot be denied its unsettling power, the apparatus of authorial control is never abandoned, and Dickens's characteristic reaction toward public executions mirrors his aesthetic concerns. Dickens's contribution to the literary debate on public hangings focuses on the difficulty of asserting control over the dissolute crowd and the degraded spectacle of the scaffold.

In a letter to Quaker philanthropist Charles Gilpin, Dickens observes "what a fearful and brutalising sight a public execution is,"[23] yet he is equally concerned with the site around the scaffold. After witnessing the execution of F. G. and Maria Manning, the first husband and wife to be executed in public together since 1700 and a major cause célèbre, Dickens declares in his letter to the *London Times* (14 November 1849), "I believe that a sight so inconceivably awful as the wickedness and levity of the immense crowd collected at that execution this morning could be imagined by no man."[24] He especially bridles at the sheer facticity of the crowd's gaze, the way "thousands upon thousands of upturned faces, so inexpressibly odious in their brutal mirth or callousness"[25] stare at the Mannings. This admonition looks forward to the denigration of the crowd's curiosity at the trial of Charles Darnay in Dickens's meditation on the French Revolution, *A Tale of Two Cities* (1859): "The sort of interest with which this man was stared and breathed at, was not a sort that elevated humanity.... Whatever gloss the various spectators put upon it, the interest was, at the root of it, Ogreish."[26] Dickens's further description of the Manning crowd would also fit comfortably in *A Tale*, with its catalogue of the crowd's "fighting, faintings, whistlings, imitations of Punch, [its] tumultuous demonstrations of indecent delight when swooning women were dragged out of the crowd by the police with their dresses disordered."[27]

Dickens's response to the crowd around the Manning execution echoes his reaction to the riotous French crowds of *A Tale of Two Cities* or the unruly mob of *Barnaby Rudge*; the crowd must be, quite literally, composed. The reader's response to the spectacle is to be guided by active intervention. In a letter detailing his proposals for the privatization of capital punishment (22 May 1858), Dickens suggests that executions be conducted in front of a specially selected "Witness jury"; executions must be restored to a pristine state, "conducted," Dickens adds, "with every terrible solemnity that careful consideration could devise."[28] The problem with modern executions is their failure to produce the proper response, as is evident in the Manning case: "Nothing would have been a greater comfort to me – nothing would have so much relieved in my mind the unspeakable terrors of the scene, as to have been enabled to believe that any portion of the immense crowd – that any grains of sand in the vast moral desert stretching away on every side – were moved to any sentiments of fear, repentance, pity, or natural horror by what they saw upon the drop."[29] "Fear," "repentance," "pity," "natural horror": the echoes of Aristotelian notions of tragic effect are evident in this delineation of what the scaffold should elicit from an audience. Mrs. Manning, Dickens observes, "had her evil passions excited to the utmost by the scene, so had all the crowd";[30] instead of offering tragic catharsis, the scaffold is "antitragic." The question is how to remedy the lack of catharsis offered by these "frightful spectacles."[31] In proposing a new practice for the scaffold, Dickens tellingly appeals to the authority of Henry Fielding's *Enquiry*. He quotes approvingly Fielding's neoclassical solution to the degraded spectacle of the public execution: "The execution should be in some degree private. And here the poets will again assist us. . . . a murder behind the scenes, if the poet knows how to manage it, will affect the audience with greater terror than if it was acted before their eyes. . . . The mind of man is so much more capable of magnifying than his eye, that I question whether every object is not lessened by being looked upon, and this more especially when the passions are concerned."[32] After citing this passage, Dickens further proposes to have "the bells of all the churches in that town or city tolled, and all the shops shut up, that all might be reminded of what was being done,"[33] echoing the concern for tragic decorum evident in Fielding's attempt to police the crowd. Dickens's suggested reforms for the privatization of executions attempt to regain control of the crowd. As such they do not differ in kind from the judgmental asides in *A Tale of Two Cities*, when the malignant gaze of the crowd at the grindstone merits the narrator's interjection that these are eyes "which any unbrutalized beholder would have given twenty years of life, to petrify with a well-directed gun."[34]

Like Dickens, William Thackeray had an avid and well-documented interest in crime, so it is no surprise that he contributed to the debate over public execution. Thackeray maintained an anxious revulsion toward executions, only attending one in his lifetime.[35] However, Thackeray's essays on capital punishment exhibit a carefully controlled, finely honed rhetoric. "The Case of Peytel" in the *Paris Sketch Book* (published 1840) exhibits a playful attention to the "fictions" of legal discourse and the rhetorical ploys justifying the scaffold; "Going to See a Man Hanged" (1840) hints at the political dangers Thackeray perceives in public execution as evident in contemporary English practice.

In "The Case of Peytel" Thackeray examines the celebrated French trial of Sebastian Peytel, a notaire executed for the murders of his wife and their servant. Thackeray's interest in the discourses surrounding law and the mechanisms of punishment, his sharp eye for the fictions of legal discourse, is evident. After quoting from the *Acte d'Accusation* on how the crime was discovered, Thackeray draws attention to the *Acte's* disruption of generic hierarchies, to the way separate genres mingle in the report; he directs his reader (and the rhetorical concern for his very English audience is apparent throughout the essay) to: "Read the first part of the Peytel act of accusation; it is as turgid and declamatory as a bad romance; and as inflated as a newspaper document, by an unlimited penny-a-liner."[36] In a dramatic flourish, he even summarizes the report of the *Proceurer's* substitute by listing the "cast of characters" of the Peytel case.[37]

As Thackeray demystifies the fictional conventions that underwrite the *Acte*, he also questions the provincial paper's report of the staid crowd at Peytel's execution—"The crowd, which had been quite silent, retired, profoundly moved by the sight it had witnessed"[38]—by contrasting his recollection of more characteristically "French" crowds. Thackeray describes at length the crowd he saw searching for Fieschi's execution, a festive crowd in the midst of "carnival time"[39] and, naturally, a morally suspect one: "a crowd of people, in hideous masquerade, drunk, tired, dirty, dressed in horrible old frippery, and daubed with filthy rouge . . . tipsy women and men, shrieking, jabbering, gesticulating, as French will do; parties swaggering, staggering forwards, arm in arm, reeling to and fro across the street, and yelling songs in chorus."[40]

Thackeray indirectly uses the behavior of the French crowd to ironize the English custom of using the execution as a disciplinary tool for children. There had been a longstanding practice of flogging children who attended public executions to reinforce the exemplary value of the spectacle.[41] Near the close of "The Case of Peytel," Thackeray describes street boys, who after witnessing Lacenaire's death, are seen dancing around "a little pool of ice, just partially tinged with red" and singing on the grounds of his execution.[42] The essay "Going to See a Man Hanged" closes with a similar episode, which also depicts the scaffold as a corruptor of youth: "As we made our way through the immense crowd, we came upon two little girls of eleven and twelve years . . . we asked the elder girl . . . what brought her into such a neighborhood? The child grinned knowingly, and said, "We've koom to see a man hanged!"[43] Finally, in "The Case of Peytel" Thackeray analyzes the urges that create such spectacles, echoing the demystifications of human behavior typical of French moralists such as La Rouchefoucauld: "it is not for moral improvement . . . that people make a holiday of a killing day"; rather, it is "a fine grim pleasure that we have in seeing a man killed."[44] Thackeray concludes: "You deter no one else from committing the crime by killing; you give us, to be sure, half an hour's pleasant entertainment."[45]

When Thackeray reports on a public execution on English soil, many of the same rhetorical devices I have just examined are used, although with a marked shift of tone. Commissioned by *Fraser's Magazine* to attend the execution of Courvoisier, a valet who murdered his master, the result is "Going to See a Man Hanged." Part of the essay's starkness can be traced to Thackeray's personal anxiety in front of the scaffold; three days after the event he writes to his mother, complaining "I have been to see Courvoisier hanged and am miserable ever since . . . it is most curious the effect his death has had on me, and I am trying to work it off in a paper on the subject."[46] When Thackeray writes of his arrival at Newgate he refuses to name the scaffold, only referring to the scaffold as "it," a small drawing of the instrument of execution the sole attempt to represent the object: "There it stands black and ready. . . . As you see it, you feel a kind of dumb electric shock."[47] Thackeray's refusal to name the scaffold has the effect of giving the unnamed object an even greater dramatic presence in the essay; it is as if to name the scaffold is to somehow deprive it of its terror. Despite his cheerful description of the jovial English crowd waiting around the scaffold, what is *not* said about the crowd dramatizes their importance in a manner similar to his dramatization of the scaffold.

True to his intention to "mingle with the crowd at the foot of the scaffold"[48] (Thackeray's eagerness to mingle is innovational in its declared denial of a distance between the narrator and the crowd), he devotes much of his essay to a description of the crowd, resembling a theatergoer's relaxed musing on the audience surrounding him before surrounding him before the play commences. As in "The Case of Peytel," Thackeray stresses the carnival nature of the crowd surrounding him; he observes that "the character of the crowd . . . was quite festive . . . jokes bandying about here and there and jolly laughs breaking out"[49] and again it is precisely the saturnalian aspect of executions that Thackeray attacks. "Government," he writes, "a Christian government gives us a feast every now and then: it agrees that for certain crimes it is necessary that a man should be hanged by the neck."[50] Thackeray maintains an internal distance if not a spatial one from the crowd; as spectator he experiences Lenten indignation in the midst of carnivalesque excess.

It does not take long for Thackeray's interpretation of the crowd to turn explicitly political. For Thackeray, the crowd that gathers around the scaffold is not a haphazard assembly; rather, it is a representative class come of age. While the Whigs and Tories have been, in his words, "jangling and brawling over accounts, Populus, whose estate [has been] administered while he was an infant, has been growing and growing, till he is every bit as wise as his guardians."[51] He continues: "In the meantime we shall continue electing and debating, and . . . having everyday new triumphs for the glorious cause of Conservativism, or the glorious cause of Reform until−."[52] Here Thackeray breaks off his "unconscionably republican tirade";[53] his sentence can only be finished by the crowd itself. The normal round of politics will continue until the crowd asserts its rights, becomes conscious of its own power. If a growing awareness of the crowd's collective strength is obvious to the general onlooker, Thackeray's persona in this essay, how could it fail to be apparent to the crowd itself? Or to the readers of *Fraser's?* The nuances of Thackeray's fragmented sentence would not have been lost on his audience; if to name the scaffold is to deprive it of its drama, then to name the crowd and its desires is to lessen the crowd's impact. The gap in Thackeray's essay reminds his audience of the crowd's inevitable entrance into politics just as the problem of penal reform is being taken up by the middle classes.

The furtive attitude toward the crowd evident in Thackeray's essay is generally lost as the public debate concerning the scaffold continues into the century. A polemical edge is apparent in the description of the crowd in the *London Times* report on Franz Muller's execution, read during Parliamentary hearings in the Commons on March 6, 1866. Muller's execution left the *Times* correspondent hoping that "such a concourse . . . may never again be assembled either for such a spectacle, or for the gratification of such lawless ruffianism as yesterday found scope around the gallows. . . . There can only be one thing more difficult than describing this crowd, and that is to forget it."[54] The secularist reformer George Jacob Holyoake echoes such rhetoric in his account of the spectators assembled at Muller's execution, relying on an image of the scaffold as the last thrill remaining for the restless sensibility of urban malcontents: "The mob was tired of melodrama. Bombast, blue lights and penny tragedies had palled on its whisky-blistered stomach. . . . It now wanted a real murder – as safe as cowardice could make it, as public as ferocity could wish it."[55] Holyoake echoes the aesthetic observations of Edmund Burke cited earlier; the crowd tires of tragic purification and demands something to satisfy the desire for constant stimulation associated with urbanism. On all sides of the public debate, a disturbing question was posed: if the scaffold had become a pretext for the disruptive workings of the crowd and, at best, a momentary diversion, what would happen when the crowd grew bored with the scaffold?

This remained a rhetorical question. Public executions officially ended in Britain in 1868, just a year after the Second Reform Bill was passed. Instead of a leveling ritual, we have an attempt to diffuse power among a broader spectrum; instead of the gibbet, we have the ballot box. Sir Edmund DuCane voiced the official consensus in *The Punishment and Prevention of Crime* (1885): "It was decided after full consideration that the scenes at a public execution were so demoralizing that they could no longer be tolerated; they collected all the scum of the neighborhood, and were little less disgusting than the former practice of the procession to the distant place of execution, while the deterrent effects were certainly no greater."[56] In Victorian fiction, the drama of urbanization echoes this move toward privatization, toward the diffusion of collective experience. The elimination of the crowd around the scaffold is paralleled by an increasing interest in the fictional delineation of individual psychology; the writer's subjective impressions of the urban scene become the new focal point. The following passage from George Gissing's *The Private Papers of Henry Ryecroft* can serve as an example. Ryecroft remembers a sleepless reverie in his garret when: "Hideous cries aroused me; sitting up in the dark, I heard men going along the street, roaring news of a hanging that had just taken place. 'Execution of Mrs.'—I forget the name of the murderess. . . . whilst I lay there in my bed, that woman had been led out and hanged—hanged. I thought with horror of the possibility that I might sicken and die in that wilderness of houses."[57] Ryecroft is the ideal imaginative "spectator" of the private execution, absented from the spectacle and from the community of onlookers, internalizing the terror of the scaffold in a fashion Fielding and Dickens would have found exemplary. A sense of the social workings behind the execution is noticeably absent from Gissing's representation of the scene. Neither the news of the execution nor its effect on the imagination of Ryecroft points toward a larger social matrix; the experience simply delineates the workings of urban anomie. Ryecroft's main worry (and the major concern that Gissing wishes to convey to his reader) is that he "might sicken and die in that wilderness of houses," in the garret where he hears the news of an execution. With the disappearance of the crowd, 19th century narrative loses, in Terry Castle's words, "a primary topoi of collective disorder,"[58] and, one should add, a way to represent social conflict and collective desires. Relinquished by the novel, film inherits this discarded trope.[59]

As for the spectacle of punishment, it has not ended, although its theatricality has long since been muted. We have moved, to use Elias Canetti's terms, from the "baiting crowd" to the detached public, informed of executions by means of the media. As Canetti writes in *Crowds and Power*: "Today everyone takes part in public executions through the newspapers. Like everything else, however it is more comfortable than it was. . . . We know more about the business than our predecessors, who may have walked miles to see it, hung around for hours, and, in the end, seen very little. The baiting crowd is preserved in the newspaper reading public, in a milder form it is true, but, because of its distance from events, a more irresponsible one."[60] We may recall Jasper Milvain's outburst at the breakfast table in *New Grub Street* and its callousness, and understand that to boast of the modern privatization of punishment as necessarily "progressive" remains premature.

Notes

1. George Gissing, *New Grub Street* (New York: Modern Library, 1925), 1.

2. Terry Castle, *Masquerade and Civilization* (Stanford, Calif.: Stanford University Press, 1986), 18. Castle's book was the initial impetus behind this essay.

3. Bernard Mandeville, *An Enquiry into the Causes of the Frequent Executions at Tyburn* (Menston, England: Scholar Press, 1971), 20.

4. Leon Radzinowicz, *A History of English Common Law*, vol. 1 (London: Stevens and Sons, 1948), 172.

5. Edmund Burke, *Works*, vol. 1 (London: George Bell and Sons, 1902), 81.

6. Peter Burke, *Popular Culture in Early Modern Europe* (London: Temple Smith, 1978), 197.

7. Robert Muchembled, *Popular Culture and Elite Culture in France, 1400-1750* (Baton Rouge: Louisiana State University Press, 1985), 208.

8. Michel Foucault, *Discipline and Punish: The Birth of the Prison*, trans. Alan Sheridan (New York: Vintage Books, 1979), 49.

9. Foucault, *Discipline and Punish*, 57.

10. James Boswell, *Boswell's Life of Johnson*, vol. 4, ed. G. B. Hill (Oxford: Clarendon Press, 1934), 188.

11. Radzinowicz, *History of English Common Law*, 1: 172.

12. Peter Burke, *Popular Culture*, 200.

13. Muchembled, *Popular Culture and Elite Culture*, 184.

14. Henry Fielding, *Complete Works of Henry Fielding, Esq.*, vol. 13 (New York: Barnes and Noble, 1967), 122.

15. Foucault, *Discipline and Punish*, 63.

16. Radzinowicz, *History of English Common Law*, 1: 171.

17. Cf. Foucault, *Discipline and Punish*, 63.

18. Georg Lukács, *The Historical Novel* (New York: Humanities Press, 1965), 23.

19. Albert Borowitz's *The Woman Who Murdered Black Satin* (Columbus: Ohio State University Press, 1981), 255-75, provides an interesting overview of the literary debate that centered on capital punishment in England during the 1840s.

20. Quoted in Philip Collins, *Dickens and Crime* (London: Macmillan, 1962), 45.

21. On Dickens's reading of urban life, see J. Hillis Miller's "The Fiction of Realism: *Sketches by Boz, Oliver Twist*, and Cruikshank's Illustrations," in *Centennial Essays*, ed. Ada Nisbet and Blake Nevius (Berkeley and Los Angeles: University of California Press, 1971), 81-155.

22. Charles Dickens, *Oliver Twist* (London: Bradbury and Evans, 1846), 308.

23. Charles Dickens, *Selected Letters of Charles Dickens*, ed. David Paroissien (London: Macmillan Press, 1985), 250.

24. Ibid., 248.

25. Ibid., 249.

26. Dickens, *A Tale of Two Cities* (New York: Grosset and Dunlap, 1940), 66.

27. Cf. *A Tale of Two Cities*, book 3, chap. 5.

28. Dickens, *Letters*, 254.

29. Ibid.

30. Ibid., 252.

31. Ibid., 253.

32. Quoted in Dickens, *Letters*, 253.

33. Dickens, *Letters*, 253.

34. Dickens, *A Tale of Two Cities*, 280.

35. William Thackeray, *The Letters and Private Papers of William Makepeace Thackeray*, vol. 5, ed. Gordon N. Ray (Cambridge: Harvard University Press, 1945–46), 718.

36. William Thackeray, "The Case of Peytel," in *The Complete Works of William Makepeace Thackeray*, vol. 5 (New York: Harper and Bros., 1898), 212.

37. Thackeray, "Peytel," 220.

38. Ibid., 230.

39. Ibid., 231.

40. Ibid.

41. Radzninowicz, *History of English Common Law*, 1: 176.

42. Thackeray, "Peytel," 232.

43. William Thackeray, "Going to See a Man Hanged," in *The Complete Works of William Makepeace Thackeray*, vol. 3 (New York: Harper and Bros., 1898), 648. Thackeray's technique is echoed in Coventry Patmore's poem, "A London Fête," included in *Poems* (London: George Bell & Sons, 1909), 424. Patmore focuses on the individual reactions by members of the crowd to the execution and gives special emphasis to the brutalizing effects the spectacle has on the young: "Mothers hold up their babes to see / Who spread their hands and crow'd for glee." This sentimental argument arises parallel with the growing realization of the failure of the public execution as pedagogic spectacle.

44. Thackeray, "Peytel," 233.

45. Ibid.

46. Thackeray, *Letters*, 1: 451–52.

47. Thackeray, "Hanging," 638.

48. Ibid.

49. Ibid., 641.

50. Ibid., 646.

51. Ibid., 640.

52. Ibid.

53. Ibid.

54. March 6, 1866, *Hansard's Parliamentary Debates*, Commons, vol. 181, p. 1623, column 2.

55. George Jacob Holyoake, *Public Lessons of the Hangman* (London: F. Farrah, 1864), 2–4.

56. Sir Edmund F. DuCane, *The Punishment and Prevention of Crime* (London: Macmillan, 1885), 24.

57. George Gissing, *The Private Papers of Henry Ryecroft* (New York: E. P. Dutton and Co., 1903), 220.

58. Castle, *Masquerade and Civilization*, 344.

59. In Siegfried Kracauer's magisterial *Theory of Film* (Oxford: Oxford University Press, 1960) he notes that where the traditional arts found themselves "unable to encompass and render" the masses, "photography easily succeeded. . . . the attraction which masses exerted on still and motion picture cameras from the outset" was readily apparent (50–51).

60. Elias Canetti, *Crowds and Power* (New York: Viking Press, 1963), 52.

"All the Hideous Apparatus of Death": Dickens and Executions

F. S. SCHWARZBACH

In *David Copperfield* there is a character named Mr. Dick who is slightly mad. He was driven mad long ago by a wicked brother-in-law who broke the heart of and (in effect) so murdered his sister, and ever since Mr. Dick has kept busy writing a "Memorial" about the injustices he has suffered. But the document is never completed, no matter how hard he labors, because whenever he sits down to write, somehow King Charles's head enters into his manuscript. He asks David the date of the king's death, and when David answers 1649, Mr. Dick responds: "So the books say; but I don't see how that can be. Because, if it was so long ago, how could the people about him have made that mistake of putting some of the trouble out of his head, after it was taken off, into mine?" (chap. 14).[1] David's aunt glosses Mr. Dick's bewilderment for David, adding that he cannot bear to recall his past pain and suffering, and somehow King Charles has come for him to represent all that. Paradoxically, he can neither confront his experience directly, nor avoid confronting it, at least in this mediated form.

Mr. Dick in many ways stands as a figure of the novelist himself (whose name he partly shares). Dickens was a man obsessed – by many things – and in his fiction he constantly alludes to the dark matters of his obsessions. Like Mr. Dick, he does so through indirect symbolic and figural representations, yet they are no less powerful as a result. A further similarity between Mr. Dick and his creator may be seen in the subject at hand, King Charles's head – the trouble with which, it probably need not be said, was that it became separated from his body in a violent manner. And, of course, one of Dickens's most powerful obsessions was with murderous violence and executions.

1

Dickens directly addressed the subject of capital punishment only twice, in a series of five articles in the *Daily News* in 1846, and again in two letters he wrote to the *London Times* in 1849.[2] But though only a few years separate them, his position changed markedly. It will be worth briefly summarizing the contents of those pieces.

The *Daily News* series grew out of a never-written essay Dickens had planned for the *Edinburgh Review* the summer before. The first was inspired by a recent execution in Ireland and argued that capital punishment served no reformative purpose; the second, published five days later, recalled witnessing the hanging of Courvoisier in 1840, when the depravity of the crowd assembled proved to him that such displays only brutalized those present. (Moreover, he said, juries often found murderers insane rather than guilty so that they should not be put to death.) Dickens went on in the succeeding letters to claim that many classes of murderers—those who acted in anger, for example—could not be deterred by fear of death, while others were encouraged in their crimes by the hope of achieving the notoriety of public execution; that statistical evidence showed that murders actually decreased when death sentences were reduced; and that the many attested cases of innocent persons wrongly executed should make us wary of ever passing the ultimate sentence. He concluded by stating firmly, "I beg to be understood as advocating the total abolition of the Punishment of Death, as a general principle, for the advantage of society, for the prevention of crime, and without the least reference to, or tenderness for any individual malefactor whatsoever."

And so the matter rested, until November 1849 when Dickens succumbed to the entreaty of a friend to watch another hanging. Dickens said at first that he had no great desire to see another such event, but the prospect of the first husband-wife execution since 1700, and the huge crowd sure to be there, were inducement enough to change his resolve, and on November 13 from a rooftop near Horsemonger Lane Gaol he saw Frederick and Maria Manning executed.[3] He was shocked—not so much at the hangings as at the demeanor of the 30,000 persons assembled to watch (one of whom, unbeknownst to Dickens, was crushed to death).

Within hours, he had written to the *Times*: "The horrors of the gib-bet and of the crime which brought the wretched murderers to it, faded in my mind before the atrocious bearing, looks and language, of the assembled spectators." Dickens saw every variety of indecent display by the children, prostitutes, and thieves gathered there, and no indication that the principal event had any effect but to occasion entertainment. He labeled public executions one "of the worst sources of general con-tamination and corruption in this country," and (alluding to a hint that the government would be willing to consider such a step) pleaded that executions should be carried out within prison walls. The letter in-stantly generated a storm of controversy.

Some, like the *Times* itself, opposed any reforms, but many friends and others who had thought Dickens an abolitionist wrote at once to register disapproval, or to urge him to make his stand more clear. That, at least, he was willing to do, and in a second, much longer letter to the *Times* he explained that private executions would have an increased deterrent effect on other criminals, while eliminating the gross inde-cency of public hangings. In personal correspondence he insisted that the desire for total abolition was premature, and to insist on it would guarantee failure of any reform.

What is not clear in all of this is whether Dickens still opposed capital punishment itself. He complained acidly about fanatics who re-jected this reform as being more likely to postpone total abolition by removing the evil from public attention, and declined to give further public support to abolitionism. Did he now reject abolition on prin-cipal, or only because it was politically ill-advised to seek it at that time? He would not say, leaving even his friends somewhat confused. The confusion he engendered is in many ways typical of his writing about these matters in his fiction as well, and it is the fiction that I wish to focus upon now.[4]

2

Murder, execution, and the execution-like deaths of murderous criminals feature prominently in nearly every novel that Dickens wrote.[5] They are there from the first—even in his first book, *Sketches by Boz* (1836), which includes "A Visit to Newgate" in which Dickens imagines the state of mind of a condemned prisoner. Nor could one imagine a novel more cheerful than his first, *Pickwick Papers* (1836–37), but even it is peppered with many horrifying varieties of violence in the interpolated tales, a series of short stories inserted in the main narrative (perhaps to make good use of material already written). In them Dickens indulges morbid imaginings banished from the largely comic world of Mr. Pickwick and his Club, albeit in lurid and badly written melodramatic accents. In one tale, for example, a man plots the murder of his wife, who is driven mad and dies when she realizes his intention; in another a transported convict returns home after many years to murder the father he believes responsible for driving him to a life of crime, only to see the old man die of a stroke as he attempts to strangle him; and in still another, a man who had watched his wife and child die in penury while his father-in-law refused them aid hounds the parent to death, along the way ensuring the death of his brother-in-law for good measure.

A modern reader might complain, as Ruskin did, that Dickens incorporated so many deaths in his fiction only to pique the jaded sensibilities of urbanites who required such horrors to rouse them from their habitual torpor.[6] It may be instructive to recall that murders in the 1830s and 1840s were comparatively rare events: in some years, there were only a bare handful, and the perpetrators were invariably brought to trial, convicted, and hanged. Hence Ruskin's complaint about the number seems in order: in *Oliver Twist* (1837–38), there is a murder, a spectacular accidental death, and an execution; in a tale in *Master Humphrey's Clock* (1840–41), an infanticide; in *Barnaby Rudge* (1841), a murder, mob violence involving scores of deaths, and a double execution; in *Martin Chuzzlewit* (1843–44), a murder, an attempted murder, and a suicide; and so on, to Dickens's last novel, the unfinished *The Mystery of Edwin Drood* (1870), which probably centers around the murder of Drood himself. Ruskin's remarks were mainly about *Bleak House* (1852–53), in which at least three characters die of fever, two more of mental exhaustion, another commits suicide, one is murdered, and another simply explodes in a gruesome instance of spontaneous combustion.

Obviously, then, Dickens's fascination with murder, murderers, and the deaths of murderers was constant throughout his writing life. And just as obviously, despite Ruskin's complaint, his fascination touched an equally strong one in his readers. We have only to recall the detailed and prominent coverage of murders and executions in the press, the extraordinary sales of broadsheets purporting to give the confessions of the condemned (in excess of 100,000 in some cases, it is said), the massive crowds who gathered at every public hanging, and the perennial attraction of murder as a subject for popular fiction (even so high-minded a writer as George Eliot used it). In search of an explanation for this phenomenon, I propose to look more closely at three of Dickens's novels—one early, one middle, and one late—in which these concerns are quite central: *Oliver Twist* (1837–39), *Martin Chuzzlewit* (1843–44), and *Our Mutual Friend* (1864–65).

3

Oliver Twist is set largely in the London criminal underworld, and quite naturally features many violent acts. Yet even that does not quite prepare the reader for the explosion of violence in the last seven chapters, which feature a brutal murder, an accidental hanging, and an execution. The murder is that of Nancy, the prostitute, by her lover, the housebreaker Bill Sikes. It is a horrifying business: Sikes resists her entreaties for mercy, and beats her on the head with his pistol butt; then, while she prays on her knees, he finishes her off with a club. The narrator solemnly declares, "Of all bad deeds that, under cover of the darkness, had been committed within wide London's bounds since night hung over it, that was the worst. Of all the horrors that rose with an ill scent upon the morning air, that was the foulest and most cruel" (chap. 48). However, despite this unequivocal pronouncement, the chapter that follows is an amazing account of Sikes's experiences over the next day and night *entirely* from his point of view. The narrator enters his consciousness completely, and in an astonishing tour de force presents his thoughts without comment or judgment.[7]

It is as if Dickens were suddenly so sympathetic to his villain that he becomes him, at least for the space of ten pages. It is a leap of fictional identification that never occurs with any of *Oliver Twist*'s virtuous characters. But this fellow feeling for the murderer vanishes as suddenly as it appears only a few pages later, when Sikes returns to London, pursued by a mob. The narrative tone is complicated by apparent authorial revulsion both from the mob and the murderer. The mob is bloodthirsty and violent; earlier Dickens had written of another mob (chasing young Oliver) that "There is a passion *for hunting something* deeply implanted in the human breast" (chap. 10; Dickens's emphasis). This mob certainly proves the point, for not only are innocent persons suffocated and crushed as it surges this way and that, but there are repeated cries that the house Sikes is in be set afire, and that the police shoot him dead. Ironically, in their effort to capture a murderer, the mob has become murderous itself.

Sikes attempts to escape by dropping from the roof to a ditch below, but slips when he imagines he sees the eyes of Nancy's corpse behind him: "Staggering as if struck by lightning, he lost his balance and tumbled over the parapet. The noose was at his neck. It ran up with his weight, tight as a bow-string, and swift as the arrow it speeds. He fell for five-and-thirty feet. There was a sudden jerk, a terrific convulsion of the limbs; and there he hung, with the open knife clenched in his stiffening hand" (chap. 50). Sikes's end at the hands of his creator is similar to other Dickens deaths, in which the novelist chooses spectacularly violent means to dispatch a villain. Quilp in *The Old Curiosity Shop* is drowned in the Thames as he seeks to escape his pursuers; some of the Gordon rioters portrayed in *Barnaby Rudge* drink burning liquor as they destroy a brewery, and so immolate themselves; Carker in *Dombey and Son* is smashed to bits by a railway locomotive; Rigaud-Blandois in *Little Dorrit* is killed when a house collapses on him; Compeyson in *Great Expectations* is drowned; and in *Our Mutual Friend* Headstone and Riderhood drown each other in the river. In all of these instances the villain is either a murderer or as bad as one (Quilp and Carker have killed no one, but have ruined several lives apiece), and in all these cases Dickens seems quite satisfied to dispose of them without benefit of trial, and without displaying mercy beforehand or pity afterward. In *Oliver Twist* Dickens even adds a particularly distasteful coda to Sikes's death: his dog tries to jump from the roof to his master's body, but falls, "and striking his head against a stone, dashed out his brains." Why the dog must pay for his owner's sins is puzzling, but it is clear that Dickens relishes the scene immensely.[8]

Similar ambiguity surrounds the death of Fagin in *Oliver Twist*. He, even more than Sikes, is described as evil incarnate, and often depicted as a reptile, coldblooded and inhuman. Yet when the narrative turns to his trial, we suddenly enter his mind, and witness the judgment and sentencing through his eyes. Even more powerful is what follows, when the reader spends "Fagin's Last Night Alive" (the chapter title) with him, or rather, in him. Again, as with Sikes after the murder, the identification is total, with no hint of authorial comment or irony. His terror is powerfully conveyed, and when he cries out, "'What right have they to butcher me?'" (chap. 52) the reader can only answer—none.

This mood ends rapidly when Oliver comes to visit Fagin, who instantly declines into a stagey caricature of temporary insanity, as if Dickens required greater distance from the character before dispatching him; but the tone shifts yet again at the very end of the chapter, when we see the lively crowd assembled to witness the execution, and the gallows itself: "Everything told of life and animation, but one dark cluster of objects in the very centre of all—the black stage, the crossbeam, the rope, and all the hideous apparatus of death." In the end, at the prospect of Fagin's end, a reader might well be forgiven some confusion about how one is meant to feel about it all.

Martin Chuzzlewit (1843–44) also features a violent murder, that of Montague Tigg by Jonas Chuzzlewit. Tigg, a swindler who has made a fortune through a fraudulent insurance company and is a blackmailer to boot, is himself hardly a model of virtue. Jonas commits the murder to cover his tracks in another, that is even worse: Tigg possesses circumstantial evidence suggesting that Jonas had poisoned his own father.[9] Whenever Dickens alludes in the narrative to Jonas's murderous intentions, he does so in terms of unequivocal condemnation, even capitalizing the phrase "Guilty Deed" (chap. 46) the better to emphasize the point. Once Tigg has been killed, all creation seems affected by it: the blood oozing from his head, Dickens writes, "dyed and scented the whole summer night from earth to Heaven" (chap. 47).

Yet again, as with Sikes, immediately after the murder is done Dickens enters the mind of the guilty man and gives us his experiences over the next day entirely from within. To be sure, the account dwells on his mental turmoil and his fear of discovery, but Dickens's profound interest in the mind of the murderer is no less remarkable. And again, as with Sikes, Dickens prefers to take justice, when it is due, into his own hands. Though Jonas is seized by the police, he takes poison during the coach ride to jail and dies horribly. The chapter in which this occurs ends thus: "They dragged him out, into the dark street; but jury, judge, and hangman could have done no more, and could do nothing now. Dead, dead, dead" (chap. 51). Perhaps having Jonas take his own life provides a means of avoiding comment on whether or not hanging is a legitimate punishment for his crime—at any rate, Dickens appears confident that no one will mourn a man who has so outraged Providence itself.

As I have noted, Dickens's fascination with murder and acts that are the moral (if not the literal) equivalent of execution is constant throughout his career. In his last completed novel, *Our Mutual Friend* (1863–65), this fascination is central both thematically and structurally. The plot revolves around several near murders, that of John Harmon and Eugene Wrayburn. The near-death experiences of Harmon and Wrayburn transform their lives utterly, ending their wasted "first" lives, and allowing them a moral and spiritual rebirth into more useful second lives. Also central is the inner state of the man who nearly kills Wrayburn, Bradley Headstone—who himself ends by drowning as he and another villain, Rogue Riderhood, attempt to kill each other.

As in *Oliver Twist* and *Martin Chuzzlewit*, it is the character of the would-be murderer, Headstone, who most interests Dickens. He is a self-made man, having by his own industry risen from humble origins to become a schoolmaster. He is, however, painfully insecure about his class and rank, and Wrayburn mercilessly torments him about them as they quarrel over Lizzie Hexam. Though Wrayburn's taunts are cruelly provocative, and though Wrayburn probably intends to ruin the woman they both love, this does not excuse Headstone's premeditated attempt to murder him. After their first encounter, Dickens writes of Headstone's "red and white heats of rage" (book 2, chap. 6), making it abundantly clear that his stiff demeanor only thinly masks a violent temper beneath. His anger intensifies at each meeting, until finally he is driven to bludgeon his victim, whom he throws into the river. (He has also attempted to cast blame on Riderhood, who while no angel is at least innocent of this particular crime.)

As one might expect, afterward Dickens presents to us Headstone's thoughts about his attack from within. (In this case, though, it is done a chapter later, and then in interrupted passages.) As before, Dickens writes with supreme confidence about what murderers must think:

> Bradley was suspicious of every sound he heard . . . but was under a spell which very commonly falls upon the shedder of blood, and had no suspicion of the real danger that lurked in his life, and would have it yet. . . . He had no remorse; but the evil-doer who can hold that avenger at bay, cannot escape the slower torture of incessantly doing the evil deed again and doing it more efficiently. . . . Bradley toiled on, chained heavily to the idea of his hatred and his vengeance, and thinking how he might have satiated both in many better ways than he had taken. (Book 4, chap. 7)

Eventually Headstone learns (as the reader already knows) that Wrayburn is not dead, but Dickens emphasizes that his lack of success was not for want of effort, and insists that the schoolmaster feels no remorse.

Perhaps it is his failure to repent, though his victim lives, that seals his doom. Indeed, Dickens almost always provides a moment when his would-be murderers have the opportunity to respond to a divine suggestion that they change their minds. In most cases, the suggestion is ignored. So, when Riderhood blackmails him about the crime, Headstone apparently decides that dying along with the only person who knows his evil secret is better than living in torment. Riderhood realizes that Headstone intends to drown him, but reminds him that having once nearly drowned he is immune (he superstitiously believes) to death by water. Headstone retorts that *he* is not: "I am resolved to be [drowned]. I'll hold you living, and I'll hold you dead. Come down!" (Book 4, chap. 15). He is as good as his word, and the two are found locked together, both quite dead. Dickens withholds comment, but the reader infers that in sentencing Riderhood and himself to death, Headstone has at least in part redeemed himself.

What is clear in all three novels is that Dickens is at least highly ambivalent about violence, even the most violent of all acts, murder itself. While he treats murder quite consistently as the most evil of all human actions, he is capable nonetheless of sympathy even for his most vicious villains, and seems to abhor execution by the state as much as the deeds that lead to the gallows. Yet he is willing himself to act as jury, judge, and executioner, and to glory self-righteously in his villains' deaths.

4

This ambivalence about murder and execution is related to a deeper and much more fundamental one, about the very nature of human nature itself. *Oliver Twist* offers particularly clear insight into Dickens's thoughts on this problem.

Early in the novel, Dickens observes of the infant Oliver, "What an excellent example of the power of dress young Oliver Twist was! Wrapped in the blanket which had hitherto been his only covering, he might have been the child of a nobleman or a beggar; it would have been hard for the haughtiest stranger to have assigned him his proper station in society. But now that he was enveloped in the old calico robes ... he ... fell into his place at once—a parish child—the orphan of the workhouse ... despised by all, and pitied by none" (chap. 1). The message, which might well have been taken from Carlyle's *Sartor Resartus*, is that society, not nature, makes us what we are in each other's eyes. The point is made many other times in the course of the novel; for example, when Noah Claypole acts brutally toward Oliver, Dickens comments, "It shows us what a beautiful thing human nature may be made to be; and how impartially the same amiable qualities are developed in the finest lord and the dirtiest charity-boy" (chap. 4). Nancy even hints that Rose Maylie, the chaste heroine, might have ended on the streets had she not had friends to care for her.

But this view of human identity as malleable (and socially determined) is not the only one Dickens presents. In the 1841 preface to the novel Dickens remarks that he had tried to show Oliver embodying "the principle of Good surviving through every adverse circumstance, and triumphing at last." It would appear, then, that some human qualities *are* innate after all. To confuse the issue even more, Oliver turns out to be of solid gentlemanly stock, and not a workhouse boy after all. (George Orwell noticed that Oliver's perfect upper-class speech indicates his true status all along.[10]) Rose (despite what Nancy says), described by the narrator as "a creature as fair and innocent of guile as one of God's own angels" (chap. 35) obviously is another such incarnation of good. The preface also alludes to "some insensible and callous natures, that do become utterly and incurably bad," like Sikes and Fagin.[11]

This contradictory view of human character as the product of nature (at times) and nurture (at other times) leads quite necessarily to some confusion about morality, and thus to confusion about crime and punishment as well. For if character is molded by social forces then society is to blame for immorality and crime. Punishment, especially the most extreme punishment—deprivation of life—must give way to rehabilitation. On the other hand, if nature is paramount over nurture, then we are innately good or evil, and (in any Christian universe) merit reward or punishment accordingly.

Such black and white contradiction, as we see in *Oliver Twist*, is most obvious in Dickens's early novels. Not so, one might think, in the middle and late fiction, justly celebrated for relentless exploration of the ways in which society determines human behavior. But, despite the novelist's insistence that social problems (e.g., ignorance, poverty, disease, the Poor Laws, etc.) cause crime, Dickens continues to present villains who seem evil by nature. For example, *Dombey and Son* has Carker (whose brother and sister appear as innately innocent as he is corrupt); *David Copperfield* has the loathsome Uriah Heep; *Bleak House* has the passionate murderess, Hortense (inspired by Maria Manning); *Little Dorrit* has Blandois-Rigaud; *Great Expectations* has Orlick, who functions as a sort of moral anti-Pip; and *The Mystery of Edwin Drood* has John Jasper, who, it has been suggested, was to have been a split personality, both good and evil warring within the same psyche.

To return for a moment to *Oliver Twist*: just after Oliver has been wrongly accused of being a pickpocket and abandoned to the justice of an angry mob by the real culprits, the Artful Dodger and Charley Bates, the narrator observes that their actions would be praised by any moral philosophers who might be watching: "the said philosophers very wisely reducing [Nature's] proceedings to matters of maxim and theory: and, by a very neat and pretty compliment to her exalted wisdom and understanding, putting entirely out of sight any considerations of heart, or generous impulse and feeling" (chap. 12). Dickens's firm faith in what Keats called "the holiness of the heart's affections," and their power to resist and redeem evil, is apparently unshakeable; yet, at the same time, the social realist in him must report behavior that indicates there is little ground for belief they will prevail. This was a paradox he never resolved.

5

If one frames Dickens's equivocations and ambivalences about violence, murder, and execution thus, then it is possible to see them as symptomatic of the prevailing Victorian uncertainty about man's place in the moral (and physical) universe in an era when rapid change was everywhere undermining traditional wisdom about the human condition. The astonishing acceleration of social and material change in the 19th century opened vociferous debate about change itself. In most simple terms, the question was this: was change merely that, or was it irreversible advancement toward if not the perfection at least the substantial amelioration of human institutions? A necessary corollary of this debate was one about human nature. For, in Christian terms, man's moral imperfectability was axiomatic; but if change indeed were progress, this could no longer be held to be so. Human character itself might advance as surely as society itself.[12]

The debate was joined in a most interesting—and for the present purpose quite relevant—essay by John Stuart Mill, boldly titled "Civilization," published in 1836. Mill begins by suggesting that the term "civilized" really means two different things: either "farther advanced in the road to perfection" or materially advanced from the state of savagery (161).[13] This allows Mill at once to rise above the partisan debate about progress, by observing that while modern England is far from barbarism in the narrow sense of the term, it is also as yet far from attaining perfection in its social and political arrangements.

Mill begins by enumerating features that distinguish civilization from barbarism: increased wealth, a greater degree of education and intelligence, more cooperation among individuals, and the rapidity with which all of the above are developing further. But Mill is concerned that in England there also "is a relaxation of individual energy" and a focusing of what remains exclusively in the realm of economic activity. The savage, he claims, must take direct action to preserve safety and liberty; the civilized man entrusts all that to "the soldier, the policeman, and the judge" (177). Only the prospect of achieving wealth calls forth endeavor in the middle classes; but among the classes already wealthy, there is nothing at all that prompts activity.

The view of modern society Mill puts forth, then, is of a materially refined but rather vitiated one. He continues:

> One of the effects of civilization (not to say one of the ingredients in it) is, that the spectacle, and even the very idea, of pain, is kept more and more out of the sight of those classes who enjoy in their fulness the very benefits of civilization. The state of perpetual personal conflict, rendered necessary by the circumstances of former times ... necessarily habituated every one to the spectacle of harshness, rudeness, and violence ... and to the alternate suffering and infliction of pain. These things, consequently, were not as revolting even to the best and most actively benevolent of men of former days, as they are to our own. ... [Today] those necessary portions of the business of society which oblige any person to be the immediate agent or ocular witness of the infliction of pain, are delegated by common consent to peculiar and narrow classes. ... We may remark too, that this is possible only by a perfection of mechanical arrangements impracticable in any but a high state of civilization. (179–80)

In other words, Mill proposes that progress toward civilization takes place not with the elimination of violence—commonplace to all in more rude societies—but with its delegation to professionals who do their work *out of sight.* (The violence itself, one notes, continues to be "necessary ... business" in civilized society.) The rest of us then can enjoy a state of great personal security and ease, but, apparently, at the cost of "moral effeminacy" (180).

The argument is strikingly prescient of Freud's ruminations in *Civilization and Its Discontents* about the fate of primitive instinct in modern man. Their common ground, it would appear, is the belief that man's violent impulses do not disappear as society advances, but are repressed in various ways. And in and through that repression, which makes civilized life as we know it possible, we both gain and lose.

Now Mill, it must be said, enjoyed a reputation in his own day as an apostle of progress, and rightly so—he (like Freud) was not advocating a return to savagery. But one senses in the mind even of this advanced atheist and materialist deep uncertainty about how (or indeed if) human nature might be perfected, and the violent impulses characteristic of "former times" eradicated. Yet it is worth noting too that Mill probably overestimated the degree of "civilization" in England in 1836: the hangings of Courvoisier in 1840 or the Mannings in 1849 attended by Dickens can hardly be termed notable examples of the delegation of violence to a few persons doing their work far from sight. Modern man was still more violent than Mill preferred to admit: and, as Dickens's responses to those very public and quite "ocular" displays of "necessary" state-inflicted violence indicate, this was a perplexing question which involved *class* as well.

After all, there were in common parlance in the 19th century "dangerous and violent classes" as well as dangerous and violent individuals. From the early 1790s the example of France was an omnipresent reminder that the lower orders, particularly in towns and cities, were potentially a revolutionary mob; their ordinary criminal tendencies might one day be channeled into a Red Terror whose horror would surpass even the foulest murder. Public hangings were in some sense a preemptive appropriation of violence to the state, preventing mass violence against it. The gallows outside Newgate served to prevent the erection of the guillotine.[14]

A case in point is Dickens's own political novel, *Barnaby Rudge* (1840), which uses a tale about the Gordon Riots of 1780 to comment on the contemporary Chartist disturbances. Dickens portrays the ancien régime as brutal and corrupt, and the mass rising in London as a quite predictable popular response to it. One of the most climactic moments is the destruction of Newgate by the mob, and the freeing of the prisoners inside, including those condemned to death. But mob violence (Dickens insists) always goes too far, and must be put down ruthlessly—in this case by the military. At the end of the novel the ringleaders are hanged; one of them, ironically, is a hangman turned rebel plotter.[15] In other words, no matter how justified the eruption of violence seems, once it has erupted Dickens's sympathy is revoked, and punishment becomes necessary.

6

Dickens's fascination with murder and execution, and his ambivalences about both, have been explained as manifestations of his peculiar and quite idiosyncratic psychological makeup. Something violent within him sought release in the fictional representation of murder, and led to his unconscious sympathy with his murderous characters, or so the argument goes.[16] Perhaps—but as I have tried to show, Dickens's equivocations and uncertainties about violence and its place in man and human institutions were by no means untypical of the Victorian era. His thinking on these most weighty matters, embodied so masterfully in his fiction, concerns questions such as: is the passion for violence an ineradicable component of the human mind? are there some persons so violent that no hope of their redemption may be entertained? and, to what extent must the state itself practice violence to prevent worse crimes? Underpinning all of these speculations is the fear that the lower classes might galvanize themselves into a revolutionary army, and unleash a Jacobin regime whose brutality would dwarf any and all heretofore known.

One should naturally be wary of any easy generalizations about an entire society, but it does seem clear that Dickens's attitudes here were far from extraordinary. What marks them as exceptional, however, is the intensity and relentlessness with which he explored these powerful, and powerfully disturbing, dilemmas. He recognized that one's response to capital punishment depends, in the end, on one's beliefs about human nature itself. We might conclude now that Dickens's moral sense about execution in the final analysis was flawed, but he did at least struggle to come to grips with it as a *moral* issue. It is the quality of his struggle, not his conclusions, that gives his fictional treatments of it the power they possess.

It is, or ought to be, unnecessary to note that more than a century later, as prisons in the United States and England bulge beyond capacity, and as calls for greater use of capital punishment are made almost daily in the Congress and Parliament, the contribution of the novelist has lost neither relevance nor value.

Notes

1. For convenience, all citations from the novels will be by chapter number in parenthesis in the text itself, thus allowing easy reference to the many editions in current circulation. The texts used are as follows: *David Copperfield*, ed. Nina Burgis (Oxford: Clarendon Press, 1981); *Oliver Twist*, ed. Kathleen Tillotson (Oxford: Clarendon Press, 1966); *Martin Chuzzlewit*, ed. Margaret Cardwell (Oxford: Clarendon Press, 1982); *Our Mutual Friend* (London: Chapman and Hall, 1865).

2. Three of the *Daily News* articles have been reprinted often, for example in the several editions of Dickens's *Miscellaneous Pieces*; another was first reprinted by Philip Collins in *The Law as Literature*, ed. Louis Blom-Cooper (London: Bodley Head, 1961), 382–87, and the fifth by Kathleen Tillotson, *Times Literary Supplement*, 12 August 1965; the *Times* letters are reprinted with extremely useful annotations in Graham Storey and K. J. Fielding, eds., *The Pilgrim Edition of the Letters of Charles Dickens*, vol. 5 (Oxford: Clarendon Press, 1981), 642 ff.

3. It may be worth noting that Dickens witnessed at least two other executions, a guillotining in Rome and a beheading in Switzerland.

4. Dickens appears to have remained sympathetic to abolition, though he made no further public statements about the issue, although there are scattered references in writings of the 1850s. By 1859, like other prominent abolitionists of the 1840s (including Carlyle), he had changed his mind, and approved of execution for murderers, though still he was in favor of making them private. When public executions were at last ended in 1868 Dickens did not comment at all, as far as we know, apparently having lost interest in the matter, along with most of the general public.

5. For a thorough, if somewhat unsympathetic, survey of Dickens's attitudes toward violence, murder, and death, see John Carey, *The Violent Effigy* (London: Faber, 1973), 11–29. See also Philip Collins, *Dickens and Crime* (London: Macmillan, 1962); Andrew Sanders, *Charles Dickens, Resurrectionist* (London: Macmillan, 1982); and Alexander Welsh, *The City of Dickens* (Oxford: Clarendon Press, 1971). I am much indebted to all of these works, from which I draw freely in my own discussion.

6. Ruskin's comments were made about *Bleak House*, but apply generally: they are in his essay, "Fiction, Fair and Foul" [which appeared originally in *The Nineteenth Century*, June 1880], *Works*, ed. E. T. Cook and Alexander Wedderburn (London: G. Allen, 1903–12), vol. 34, 270–72.

7. In the late 1860s when Dickens created a public reading version of the murder, he added three pages of entirely new material that feature more of Sikes's experiences portrayed from within the murderer's mind, including his thoughts just before the moment of his death.

8. Years later Dickens wrote a headline for the page on which this scene is depicted—"The Wild Beast Laid Low"—which emphasizes Sikes's subhuman nature, as if to justify further his violent death.

9. In fact Jonas has not, but ironically believes he is guilty of the awful act, about which he has no remorse at all. This, of course, makes his one genuine murder unnecessary, a fact Jonas learns only after he is arrested for it.

10. See Orwell's essay, "Charles Dickens," in *Inside the Whale and Other Essays* (London: Victor Gollancz, 1940), 46.

11. The conflicting views of human nature in the novel are discussed in Rosemarie Bodenheimer, *The Politics of Story in Victorian Social Fiction* (Ithaca: Cornell University Press, 1988), 120–30.

12. An early, classic round in the debate is Robert Southey's *Colloquies* (1829) and Thomas Macaulay's review of it in the *Edinburgh Review* (1830). Southey compares favorably to his own England that of Sir Thomas More; Macaulay's searing riposte makes the case for material and social progress as persuasively as ever was made in the 19th century. Another useful compendium of contemporary speculation on the question of progress, human nature, and God is Tennyson's *In Memoriam A.H.H.* (1850).

13. The essay appeared originally in the *London and Westminster Review*. The text I use is taken from Mill's *Dissertations and Discussions* (London: John W. Parker, 1859), vol. 1. Further references are by page number in parenthesis in the body of the essay. It may be of interest to note that Mill, who like Dickens was opposed to capital punishment in the 1830s and 1840s, eventually came to support it, voting against abolition as a member of parliament in the 1860s. (I am indebted to Steven Marcus for first calling Mill's essay to my attention.)

14. Thackeray's essay, "Going to See a Hanging" (originally published in *Fraser's Magazine*, 1840, and variously reprinted), also a response to witnessing the execution of Courvoisier, makes this point with astonishing clarity; see the discussion of it in Barry Faulk's essay in the present volume, a version of which I was fortunate to read before submitting my own.

15. The pattern of the novel—a brutal and repressive political order virtually forces the populace to rebel, but the rebellion almost at once exceeds legitimate bounds and must be suppressed violently—is repeated in the later *A Tale of Two Cities* (1859). (See the discussion of this in Raymond Williams, *Culture and Society* ([London: Chatto and Windus, 1958], 87–109.) There are also in this pattern some significant similarities to Dickens's portrayal of murderers—sympathetic, up to a point, but not so far as to prevent him from violently dispatching them to punish their crime.

16. The degree to which Dickens identifies with murderers—and what they may indicate about his own personality—is discussed brilliantly by Edmund Wilson in "Dickens: The Two Scrooges," in *The Wound and the Bow*

(Boston: Houghton Mifflin, 1941), and variously reprinted. Also of relevance here is Dickens's obsession with performing a condensed version of the murder in *Oliver Twist*, "Sikes and Nancy," during his last reading tours. Dickens's reading had a most powerful effect upon his audiences and upon his own health, and the claim that he brought about his own death by too frequent performances of it is only slightly exaggerated. For a review of the available evidence, see Philip Collins, ed., *Charles Dickens: The Public Readings* (Oxford: Clarendon Press, 1975), 465–71.

The Execution of Tess d'Urberville at Wintoncester

BETH KALIKOFF

Thomas Hardy witnessed two hangings in his youth. Only the second is detailed in the autobiographical biography he constructed with Florence Emily Hardy. In the summer of his eighteenth year Hardy was studying architecture at the Dorchester office of Mr. Hicks. Before walking to work from Bockhampton, Hardy would rise and read from 5:00 A.M. to 8:00 A.M. ("if *Early Life* is to be believed," comments his biographer Michael Millgate).[1] One morning he "remembered that a man was to be hanged at eight o'clock at Dorchester":

> He took up the big brass telescope that had been handed on in the family, and hastened to a hill on the heath a quarter of a mile from the house, whence he looked towards the town. The sun behind his back shone straight on the white stone facade of the gaol, the gallows upon it, and the form of the murderer in white fustian, the executioner and officials in dark clothing and the crowd below being invisible at this distance of nearly three miles. At the moment of his placing the glass to his eye the white figure dropped downwards, and the faint note of the town clock struck eight.[2]

Similarly, at the end of *Tess of the d'Urbervilles* "the hour had struck" and the reader observes an awful justice from a distance.[3] Hardy "seemed alone on the heath with the hanged man, and crept homeward wishing he had not been so curious" (Florence Hardy 29). This is a further cry from the effect of execution on Tess's husband and sister, who remain close to the earth "as if in prayer" before summoning the strength to go on (542).

In this essay I wish to explore the cultural resonance of public execution in Thomas Hardy's late–Victorian classic, *Tess of the d'Urber-villes* (1891). Memories of the first execution Hardy witnessed, that of Martha Browne in 1856 when he was 16, retained their grim power for him 60 years later, as his letters and biographers testify. His remarkable recollection of the vivid, erotically charged details of Browne's death are, unsurprisingly, absent from the account given to Florence Hardy in the *Life* on which they collaborated. But they cast another shadow over the grimly allusive scene of Tess's execution.

A less familiar and more provocative influence on the conclusion of *Tess* is that of popular gallows literature. The motifs of Hardy's poems, as J. Hillis Miller points out, attest to the way his "imagination is stirred by churchyards, gravestones, funerals, coffins, passing-bells, ghosts, skeletons"; moreover, many of his narrators speak from beyond the grave.[4] A battalion of scholars, including Donald Davidson, Deborah Greenhill, Harold Orel, and Maire A. Quinn, have discussed the influence of folk ballads and culture on Hardy's work.[5] I would like to suggest that the literary and iconographic conventions of gallows street literature mingle with the folk and classical allusions in *Tess*, shedding light on the female hero as criminal and the power of public execution to kindle the literary imagination a generation after the final spectacle in 1868.

1

Executions in Victoria's England provided the public with the op-portunity, instructive or otherwise, to watch a criminal punished by death amidst a "carnival atmosphere" of street preachers and ballad hawkers, friends and strangers.[6] The promise of seeing a particularly notorious murderer hanged—Maria Manning, for example, in 1849—drew many thousands of people who traveled to the event on specially scheduled trains. Watching criminals killed by justice became a kind of blood sport considered appropriate for men and women of all classes.[7] Sometimes school was cancelled so that "young gentlemen could absorb a wholesome lesson from beholding the demise of a wrongdoer."[8]

The "lesson" of public execution also exercised a powerful grip on the 19th century literary imagination. William B. Thesing explores "the poetry of hanging" in verse by William Wordsworth, Coventry Patmore, and A. E. Housman. Barry Faulk analyzes the social dynamic of public execution and its effect on William Thackeray. And F. S. Schwarzbach illuminates the influence of public hanging on that aficionado of Victorian crime, Charles Dickens. Thomas Hardy was one of the many Victorian writers—the famous as well as the anonymous—who were moved by the grotesque spectacle of public execution.

Significantly, Florence Hardy's work glosses over the hanging that Hardy saw at 16, mentioning the event only in the context of the execution detailed above. Yet the first hanging he saw proved even more disturbing: it was "that of a woman two or three years earlier, when he stood close to the gallows" (Florence Hardy 29). Hardy was among the three or four thousand people who attended the execution of Martha Browne on August 9, 1856 (Millgate 63), and he was only some yards rather than three miles from the scaffold on that occasion. His 1926 letter to Lady Hester Pinney clarifies this notable absence of detail in *The Life*.

"I remember what a fine figure she showed against the sky as she hung in the misty rain," Hardy writes, "& how the tight black silk gown set off her shape as she wheeled half-round & back."[9] Millgate quotes a strikingly vivid detail: "Hardy recalled on another occasion, 'I saw—they had put a cloth over the face—how, as the cloth got wet, *her features came through it*. That was extraordinary'" (63). As Harold Orel observes in *The Unknown Thomas Hardy*, these details still retain the power to startle us with their "note of subdued erotic appreciation" (129).

The causal connection of Victorian women's sexuality to their violent deaths has been explored by a range of scholars, but it may be helpful to make a few additional comments. Browne was executed for killing her young husband in a jealous rage. Tess's murder of Alec d'Urberville springs from more complex motives, delineated by Hardy with moving clarity, but she is linked to Browne and other notorious women murderers by the extremity of her beauty and her passion. For many Victorian observers, the comeliness of women killers was increased or even created by the knowledge of their criminal passions, furious or erotic or both. As Albert Borowitz points out in his study of Manning, "one of the appropriate definitions of a 'beauty' in the dictionary of the English language would be 'any accused murderess, particularly when wearing a veil.'"[10]

Like Manning, "the woman who murdered black satin" for the respectable by wearing it in court and on the scaffold, Browne is elegantly dressed, provoking spectators to consider her mortal body before her spirit is jerked from its earthly trials. Similarly, Tess's body throughout the novel provokes men to watch her. In turn Hardy depicts the corporeal Tess with the eye of a father, a lover, and a painter. She awakens at Stonehenge to discover a ring of male spectators staring at her, a grim foreshadowing of the spectators at her execution.

That Hardy is stimulated by the incongruous simultaneity of Browne's veil—the way it conceals and reveals her features—may well resonate through his depiction of Tess as both generic, a field-woman becoming one with the field, and tragically individual. In this context, Hardy's account of himself as having remained a child until he was 16 seems to signal more than the importance of leaving school and beginning his articles (Millgate 57). Watching the state execute a passionate woman becomes a male rite of passage, a violent, erotic experience that wrests a boy from childhood. Years later, Hardy has Angel Clare and Liza Lu—"half girl, half woman" (541)—seared together by seeing Tess hang. After this shocking rite, "Their pale faces seemed to have shrunk to half their natural size," and they walk on hand in hand, a crushed Adam and Eve expelled from the Garden.

2

Hardy was influenced by popular literature as well as by his formative memories of witnessing two executions. Murder, like bigamy, is a familiar plot device in sensation novels (Altick 83). Joan Grundy detects "a family resemblance" between Hardy's fiction and Victorian melodrama.[11] *Desperate Remedies* shares plot twists with *Lady Audley's Secret* and perhaps with *Maria Marten*, while the central situation of *The Colleen Bawn* "has a very general affinity with that of *Tess*" (86–87). Desmond Hawkins adds that the choice of Stonehenge for the site of

Tess's arrest demonstrates that "Hardy was a true Victorian when it came to the use of bold melodramatic effects."[12] Indeed, Hardy's original title for the novel when it was published in magazine form was "Too late, Beloved!" Later he removed the comma, leaving the title more ambiguous but still melodramatic (*Letters* 189).

The influences of melodrama and sensational fiction are evident in Hardy's work, but the strongest popular influence is held to be that of folk ballads, tales, and music. One critic says that Hardy's ballads represent his most numerous and varied use of his notebooks and memories.[13] Another notes that this creative appropriation of the ballad informs the novels as well as the poetry; there are plentiful examples of rustic characters like Joan Durbeyfield singing folk ballads, and *The Dynasts* was first conceived "as a ballad, or group of ballads" (Davidson 14). Hardy's use of folk music has been similarly explored by critics.

Like melodrama, sensation fiction, and folk ballads, gallows street literature offers literary critics insight to the study of Hardy's *Tess*. This rich subgenre also provides cultural historians with another key to some of the effects of public execution on the Victorian imagination. Richard Altick and Michael Hughes are among the scholars who have contributed to our understanding of the role of gallows literature in 19th century culture. These broadside accounts of murderers condemned to be hanged were, Hughes tells us, the most popular form of street literature, outselling other kinds by a wide margin.[14] Although the popularity of these inexpensive broadsides faded in the 1870s with the increased accessibility of newspapers, they were thriving in Hardy's late adolescence, the period when he developed "a horrified fascination with the great city."[15]

The conventions of gallows literature owe as much to fiction as to journalism. Many broadsides include verse or prose criminal confessions. When genuine confessions were not forthcoming, balladeers and writers made them up. The same is true of the letter from the criminal to his wife or sweetheart. Richard Altick offers a composite: "Dear – – –, Shrink not from receiving a letter from one whom is condemned to die as a murderer. Here, in my miserable cell, I write to one whom I have, from my first acquaintanceship, held in the highest esteem. . . ." (49). Most examples of gallows literature will include a prose account of the murder itself, a prose or verse confession, and a description of the criminal's execution, complete with final words (Altick 48). Some feature the death-cell letter or ballad Altick recreates. The broadsides I have read almost always conclude with prosaic details of crowd size, train schedules, and local addresses (16), as if to emphasize the pedestrian as well as the grotesque and to place the event in the context of other leisure activities.

The woodcut that de rigueur begins the broadsides offers a graphic depiction of the murder or the execution (Altick 50). Those that present the moment when killers are "cast into eternity" are the most useful for deepening our understanding of Tess's death. Although each street merchant claimed to be selling broadsides that displayed a distinctive picture of the killer in the act or on the scaffold, in fact the same woodcuts were used over and over for any number of broadsides. Charles Hindley's collection of street literature shows the same woodcut for the 1786 execution of Joseph Richards as for that of Michael Barrett, the last person to be publically executed, in 1868.[16]

In this archetypal scene, the gallows rises from the background, centered between a white church on the left and a black prison on the right. The criminal's hands are bound behind his back, and his features are obscured by a white bag or cloth. Filling the foreground are spectators in silhouette, distinguished from each other only by quickly cut hats, shawls, bonnets. They face the scaffold in such great numbers that there is no ground visible between church and prison, only a sea of dark spectators.

How do we move from this crude woodcut to the evocative ending of Hardy's tragedy? Unlike the faceless spectators in the woodcut or youthful Hardy at Browne's execution, the reader remains outside the prison walls. Tess, that most sensual of late-Victorian characters, is bodiless, invisible. We see no crowds, either in carnival or solemn mood, only Tess's husband and sister, moving slowly from the execution up the hill. Our initial comparison suggests that even if Hardy remembered the gallows literature of his youth, he sequestered that memory beyond the reader's imaginative reach, as though it were imprisoned in an "ugly flat-topped octagonal tower," a "blot" on the cold aesthetic beauty of the final pageant (542).

3

Tess of the d'Urbervilles leads inexorably to the gallows. The doomed inevitability with which Tess herself moves toward Wintoncester Hardy compares explicitly to that of Greek tragedy. But his readers would also have recognized the equally fated (if more monotonous) narrative drive of gallows literature: seduced and betrayed, child out of wedlock, poverty and exhaustion, death and dishonor. At the end of the novel, Tess "is once more the deserted maiden who finally murders her seducer with a knife in the effective ballad way" (Davidson 17). In criminal broadsides women who kill their betrayers earn a kind of sympathy, but from a safe distance: they have already determined their fatal destinies. So Tess "herself is the second victim of her desperate rage against the man who has torn her life to pieces."[17] The "cheerful ballad about a murder" that the dairy folk sing earlier, as Angel carries Tess across a stream, to their mutual delight, is not merely ironic, as Marlene Springer suggests, but prophetic in its connection of sexual pleasure and violent death.[18] This inexorability creates an echo of broadside symmetry and even broadside justice.

Tess is criminal from the beginning of the novel. A member of a morally bankrupt aristocratic family, Tess is like a child born to a mother in prison. "The nature she inherits," argues J. Hillis Miller, "forces her to enact involuntarily a new version of a life which has been lived over and over again by her ancestors." She tries not to know her past, or to forget what she knows, but "her forebodings are fulfilled when she kills Alec," an act predestined by "the family tradition of the coach and murder" (103).

Being born a woman is as criminal as being born a d'Urberville. That is why, as Elizabeth Ermarth observes, Tess must endure "exploitation on her family's behalf and separation from her husband."[19] A fallen woman, in this context a grimly repetitive phrase, Tess can only rise to the scaffold. One contemporary reviewer expressed contempt for this final irony: "She rises through seduction to adultery, murder, and the gallows. Higher than the gallows, indeed, this frail nature of ours is often incapable of rising while lodged in its earthly tenement."[20] As the crimes of seduced murderers are reduced to a "cycle of rebellion and submission" in street literature (Williams 845), so Tess participates in the ritual of crime and punishment at her last meeting with Alec: "Now punish me!" she said, turning up her eyes to him with the hopeless defiance of the sparrow's gaze before its captor twists its neck. "Whip me, crush me; you need not mind those people under the rick. I shall not cry out. Once a victim, always victim: that's the law" (453). This final encounter "is a portrait of her fate in miniature,"[21] just as the staring eyes at Stonehenge preview the spectators at her execution. D. H. Lawrence observes that finally Tess has come to side "with the community's condemnation of her."[22] In her despair there are echoes of the singsong warning of gallows literature: "Oh come all you ladies fair and hearken well to me. . . ."

Criminal and penitent, seduced and betrayed, Tess may lack the predictable rhetoric of gallows literature, but her journey to her own hanging resonates with the archetypal voices of the broadside women whose fate she shares. As the novel reaches its tragic conclusion, readers are removed from the flesh-and-blood dairymaid and her pain to a literary version of the broadside woodcut. Tess becomes spectacle.[23]

Arlene Jackson argues in her fine study that Hardy's pictorial rhetoric has a powerfully antirealistic effect.[24] The way he freezes a visual frame—at Stonehenge, for example—causes characters and actions to become static while emphasizing "the grotesque effects of his plotting techniques" (10). Jackson observes that "With the staticism of picture, human action becomes carved in the manner of a woodcut: flesh and blood human warmth becomes either sculptured, or framed, or set into position for display," estranging us (10).

The grotesque flatness of a woodcut is the iconographic equivalent of the pictorial rhetoric that removes Tess from the eyes of the reader. We do not see her hanged. We do not need to. Instead, as spectators, we note the church and the jail, the black flag ascending the tower, the two gazers, whose faces are as anonymous as those in street literature. No wonder that the famous allusion seems strangely displaced: "'Justice' was done, and the President of the Immortals (in Aeschylean phrase) had ended his sport with Tess" (542). As the final scenes move to the gallows with a cold and stately grace, execution becomes pageant, just, wooden, final. Even as we are moved by Tess's story we are estranged from its symmetrical denouement. Hardy's commentary "belongs to another order of discourse," one in which, as Dorothy Van Ghent tartly observes, "young girls make ameliorated lives out of witness of a sister's hanging."[25]

The public execution of Tess d'Urberville lacerates and bonds the two gazers on the hill. It completes an inexorable cycle of crime and punishment. Lastly, it symbolizes the sacrificial process by which persecutors turn victims into symbols not only of violence—in this case violent passions—but of peace and order as well.[26] Almost 30 years after the hanging of Michael Barrett and 60 years after the hanging of Martha Browne, Hardy was still moved by the spectre of public execution. With the conclusion of *Tess of the d'Urbervilles* he created a scene that owes as much to the cultural memory of gallows literature as to that of Greek tragedy.

Notes

1. Michael Millgate, *Thomas Hardy: A Biography* (New York: Random House, 1982), 63.
2. Florence Emily Hardy, *The Life of Thomas Hardy* (1962; rpt. Hamden, Conn.: Archon Books, 1970), 28.
3. Thomas Hardy, *Tess of the d'Urbervilles* (1891; rpt.; ed. Juliet Grindle and Simon Gatrell, Oxford: Clarendon Press, 1983), 542. All further references to the novel are to this edition.
4. J. Hillis Miller, *Thomas Hardy: Distance and Desire* (Cambridge: Harvard University Press, 1970), 223.
5. Donald Davidson, "The Traditional Basis of Thomas Hardy's Fiction," in *Hardy: A Collection of Critical Essays*, ed. Albert J. Guerard (Englewood Cliffs, N.J.: Prentice-Hall, 1963), 10–23; Deborah Greenhill, "'Sing That Ballad Again!': Thomas Hardy and the Traditional Ballads," *Folklore and Mythology Studies* 4 (1980): 33–46; Harold Orel, *The Unknown Thomas Hardy: Lesser-Known Aspects of Hardy's Life and Career* (Brighton, England: Harvester Press, 1984); Maire A. Quinn, "Hardy as Balladist: The Sacrilege," *Thomas Hardy Yearbook* 6 (1976): 28–29.
6. Daniel E. Williams, "'Behold a Tragic Scene Strangely Changed into a Theater of Mercy': The Structure and Significance of Criminal Conversion Narratives in Early New England," *American Quarterly* 38, no. 5

(1986): 827–47. Williams's description also holds true for executions that took place in Victorian England.

7. I discuss the way public hanging, in gallows literature, functions as sport and entertainment in *Murder and Moral Decay in Victorian Popular Literature* (Ann Arbor, Mich.: UMI Research Press, 1986), chap. 1.

8. Richard D. Altick, *Victorian Studies in Scarlet* (New York: Norton, 1970), 111.

9. *The Collected Letters of Thomas Hardy*, ed. Richard Little Purdy and Michael Millgate (Oxford Clarendon Press, 1988), 7: 5.

10. Albert Borowitz, *The Woman Who Murdered Black Satin: The Bermondsey Horror* (Columbus: Ohio State University Press, 1981), 12.

11. Joan Grundy, *Hardy and the Sister Arts* (London: Macmillan Press, 1979), 61.

12. Desmond Hawkins, *Hardy: Novelist and Poet* (Newton Abbot, Devon, England: David & Charles, 1976), 136.

13. Dennis Taylor, *Hardy's Poetry 1860–1928* (London: Macmillan Press, 1981), 97.

14. Foreword to *Curiosities of Street Literature*, ed. Charles Hindley (1871; rpt. ed. New York: Augustus M. Kelley, 1970), 9.

15. Philip Collins, "Hardy and Education," in *Thomas Hardy: The Writer and His Background*, ed. Norman Page (New York: St. Martin's Press, 1980), 50.

16. *Curiosities of Street Literature* (1871; rpt. ed. New York: Augustus M. Kelley, 1970), 176, 228.

17. Frank R. Giordano, Jr., *"I'd Have My Life Unbe": Thomas Hardy's Self-Destructive Characters* (University: University of Alabama Press, 1984), 180.

18. Marlene Springer, *Hardy's Use of Allusion* (Lawrence: University Press of Kansas, 1983), 129.

19. Elizabeth Ermarth, "Fictional Consensus and Female Casualties," in *The Representation of Women in Fiction*, ed. Carolyn G. Heilbrun and Margaret R. Higonnet (Baltimore: Johns Hopkins University Press, 1983), 12.

20. Mowbray Morris, "Culture and Anarchy," in *Thomas Hardy: The Critical Heritage*, ed. R. G. Cox (New York: Barnes and Noble, 1970), 218.

21. Perry Meisel, *Thomas Hardy: The Return of the Repressed* (New Haven: Yale University Press, 1973), 133.

22. D. H. Lawrence, "Predilection d'artiste," in *Hardy: A Collection of Critical Essays*, ed. Albert J. Guerard (Englewood Cliffs, N.J.: Prentice-Hall, 1963), 51.

23. Kaja Silverman, "History, Figuration, and Female Subjectivity in *Tess of the d'Urbervilles*," *Novel: A Forum on Fiction* 18, no. 1 (1984): 24.

24. Arlene Jackson, *Illustration and the Novels of Thomas Hardy* (Totowa, N.J.: Rowman and Littlefield, 1981), 9.

25. Dorothy Van Ghent, "On *Tess of the d'Urbervilles*," in *Hardy: A Collection of Critical Essays*, 79.

26. René Girard, "Generative Scapegoating," in *Violent Origins: Ritual Killing and Cultural Formation*, ed. Robert G. Hamerton-Kelly (Stanford: Stanford University Press, 1987), 92.

The Frame for the Feeling: Hangings in Poetry by Wordsworth, Patmore, and Housman

WILLIAM B. THESING

To examine poetry written during the hundred year period between 1836 and 1936 in England is to witness a change in the very function of the poetic art in society. Analyzing the images, structures, patterns, statements, and ambitions recorded by William Wordsworth, Coventry Patmore, and A. E. Housman in poems that treat the subject of hangings, it becomes apparent that developments of significance took place over the century. Poetry written with high political purpose yielded to a poetry with more personal applications of political ideas. Although David Cooper and Beth Kalikoff have written some important criticism on the role of popular broadsides about murderers and executions, it remains to assess the role that poets of the high literary tradition played in recording and responding to the fact of hangings during this period.[1] Of the three poets treated here, one held the title of poet laureate (Wordsworth, 1843–1850) and one was a serious candidate for the position (Coventry Patmore, in 1892). These poets were at the other end of the literary spectrum from the popular broadside writers who commemorated public hangings and in some cases registered social protests. Some larger questions to be asked include: Did poets feel that poetry could or should address such important social issues as capital punishment? Did they employ different strategies or patterns of imagery? Did they express emotional statements of lasting importance concerning the life-and-death matter of a hanging ordered by society's justice and laws? What did they conceive the nature and function of poetry to be? How did their poems function in the cultures in which they were written and read?

1

As Donald J. Gray has pointed out in introductory essays to his anthology *Victorian Literature: Poetry*, the grand conception of a poet's role in society was part of the romantic legacy passed on to the Victorians. Wordsworth's presence on the literary scene of early Victorian England in the 1830s and 1840s helped to shape the conceptions of Victorian poets and poetry. Wordsworth was recognized and lionized as a major poet during the early Victorian decades in which he published his last poems. In these years especially, he used poetry to give point to moral and political statements. Wordsworth spoke from a position of eminence; the poet had a special responsibility as prophet or spiritual leader in his society. As Gray observes: "Victorian poems and poets did act, directly and indirectly, on the consciousness and will of people who, whether they read them or not, lived in a society that publicly honored poets."[2]

In the last two decades of his life Wordsworth was an important presence on the literary scene. By the mid-1830s he was making a significant and steady income from the writing of poetry. Readers in increasing numbers purchased his volumes between 1835 and 1850. In 1842 he was awarded a government pension and in 1843 he was appointed poet laureate. While he made infrequent trips from his home in the secluded Lake District to London, he did write and talk about such current issues as the copyright law, capital punishment, the law regulating public assistance to the poor, and the impact of towns and machinery on the imaginative life of human beings, and his thoughts on these and other issues were highly regarded. A key idea to Wordsworth was that poetry should bring and spread harmony. To Wordsworth, the purpose and effect of a poem is "to rectify intellectual, moral, and even social and political disorder by literally creating order and, more important, the pleasure of order in the lives of humans."[3] In his latter years Wordsworth was absolutely sure of the *high* purposes of his poems. In 1839–40 he wrote and published 14 deliberately argumentative sonnets that endorsed capital punishment. As Gray stresses, "he wrote his poems to make a difference in the life of his time." Further evidence of Wordsworth's ambitious outlook concerning poetry's mission in the world can be found in his letters and in his "Prelude" to the volume of new and old poems that he published in 1842, wherein he sends his poems as consolation and exhortation into the wind of social, political, and moral distress. He hopes that his poems will bring order and spread harmony in society. In sum, Wordsworth insisted that "a poet must be continually and centrally present in his culture."[4] On these terms, Wordsworth is significant as an example and as a measuring stick for other poets who took up the calling of poet in the decades following his life.

The 14 sonnets by Wordsworth were written in response to a debate in Parliament in 1836 over a proposal to reduce the extensive number of crimes for which the death penalty could be imposed. Wordsworth opposed what was then regarded as an extreme or wildly liberal argument that capital punishment should be abolished for *all* crimes *except* treason and murder. In 1837 a series of criminal law reforms were proposed by the Whig government. Wordsworth did not oppose the bills of 1837, but he strongly opposed the trend toward *total* abolition of capital punishment. He felt very strongly that for the crimes of treason and murder the ultimate penalty was necessary. Wordsworth was moved to write poetry about these public events and to consider the moral questions that they involved. He composed the series of sonnets in 1839 and 1840; they were first published as part of a review essay on Wordsworth's poetry written by Sir Henry Taylor in the *Quarterly Review* in December 1841.[5] In the tradition of "high argument" he explains his reasons and attempts to persuade readers of the legitimacy of his opinions by appealing to both reason and feeling. At this point in his career, Wordsworth was 71 years old; he commanded the respect given a venerable sage. By employing the devices of poetry—imagery, a meditative sequence—he can more effectively persuade his readers to accept his position than if he had (as writers such as Henry Mayhew and others did) chosen to express his views on the social issue in an expository prose pamphlet.

Very little critical discussion of Wordsworth's 14 sonnets on the issue of capital punishment exists. However, Seraphia D. Leyda in "Wordsworth's *Sonnets Upon the Punishment of Death*" offers a detailed discussion of the poems and categorizes them into several groups for analysis.[6] There are two limitations to her essay that need to be addressed here: her line-by-line and poem-by-poem focus overlooks the effect of the larger pattern of images employed by Wordsworth, and she does not refer to other poems in the Wordsworth canon that employ images of gallows.

In his 1841 review essay Taylor identified a unique feature of Wordsworth's sonnet series on punishment by death. He praised the poems for their mixture of feeling and thought, their quality of "imaginative reason." On the ethical or rational level, Wordsworth deals with various complexities of the issue. For example, in the fifth sonnet the poet rejects the idea that the state has no right to exact the forfeiture of life and in the eleventh and twelfth sonnets he rejects the alternatives of secondary punishment—solitary imprisonment or transportation to a colony such as Australia. Equally significant—and what accounts for the special achievement of Wordsworth making his case through the medium of poetry—are the sonnets that create and intertwine images and dwell on states of feeling. Thus, society's penalty of death is reinforced by symbols that are associated with tradition and patriarchy. The first sonnet describes the "grey towers" of Lancaster Castle.[7] The emblems of patriarchy in the form of the tower, the great edifice, and the lord are those of a solid strength and confident social order that reaches back to medieval times. The aura of the site is impressive:

SUGGESTED BY THE VIEW OF LANCASTER CASTLE (ON THE ROAD FROM THE SOUTH)

> This Spot—at once unfolding sight so fair
> Of sea and land, with yon grey towers that still
> Rise up as if to lord it over air—
> Might soothe in human breasts the sense of ill,
> Or charm it out of memory; yea, might fill
> The heart with joy and gratitude to God
> For all his bounties upon man bestowed:
> Why bears it then the name of "Weeping Hill"? (p. 405)

The answer to the question posed in the sonnet's last line is swift: because thousands of prisoners have been led in chains to the top of the fortress-prison to weep and meet their executions. By mixing the strength of the tower, by suggesting the centuries of tradition behind the castle-prison, Wordsworth lends an authority to the place of punishment. He also considers the reader's natural emotional response by softening the scene with the balancing tendencies of sympathy and compassion for the criminals. The indulgence in sentiment in the final two lines of the first sonnet is overwhelming in its emotional power: "blinded as tears fell in showers / Shed on their chains: and hence that doleful name" (p. 405).

One of the key discoveries in Beth Kalikoff's *Murder and Moral Decay in Victorian Popular Literature* is the close association that literature reveals between murder and sexuality. Male-female polarities more often than not were a part of crime and justice as it was depicted in popular literature of the Victorian period. A similar, but sometimes more muted, tendency can be found in poems by writers of the "high" literary tradition. In arriving at his philosophical and ethical arguments for the death penalty, for example, Wordsworth in the four sonnets, IX, X, XI, and XII asks the rhetorical question "What is a state?" He replies that the wise "behold" in the state "A creature born of time, that keeps one eye / Fixed on the statutes of Eternity" (p. 406). As Leyda explains, "With his usual benign sexism, Wordsworth personifies this creature, the State, as a female. Like an obedient daughter, 'her judgments reverently defer' to the statutes of Eternity, while as a dutiful wife she gives birth from her inner being to the 'idea' of the State, by speaking dispassionately through Law."[8] In another significant "spots of time" passage in Book 12 of *The Prelude* that Leyda does not discuss in her essay, Wordsworth uses the male-female principles to an even greater extent to weave his poetic images.

In Book 12 of *The Prelude* – a poem whose single subject is the development of Wordsworth's sensibilities – a haunting scene is described that makes a lasting effect on the young poet's ethical nature. Wordsworth defined "spots of time" as heightened moments of insight and awareness that could be recaptured years later and then provide "A renovating virtue" (p. 577). In this instance, Wordsworth as a solitary wanderer in the Lake District comes upon the remains of a gallows edifice that had been used years earlier to execute a murderer. He recalls that at length he

> Came to a bottom, where in former times
> A murderer had been hung in iron chains.
> The gibbet-mast had mouldered down, the bones

And iron case were gone; but on the turf,
Hard by, soon after that fell deed was wrought,
Some unknown hand had carved the murderer's name.
The monumental letters were inscribed
In times long past; but still, from year to year,
By superstition of the neighbourhood,
The grass is cleared away, and to this hour
The characters are fresh and visible:
A casual glance had shown them, and I fled,
Faltering and faint, and ignorant of the road. (pp. 577–78)

For the adolescent Wordsworth, the oppression of the scene is over-whelming. The masculine principle of societal justice is total and powerful: society demands ultimate punishment for murderers and the remaining edifice and huge letters proclaim the triumph of patriarchal justice, the unrelenting letter of the law. But again, Wordsworth softens his view with an immediate and dramatic shift in perspective. He turns his eyes from this scene of the just sacrifice to the contemplation of a balancing feminine principle. On the hill above the sight there is the figure of a young girl walking in the wind. In contemplating the girl's movements, Wordsworth moves from a rational, literal state of mind to a spiritual and emotional realm of "visionary dreariness." Years later the effect of the incident is to mingle the somber pain of the criminal's memory with the revivifying pleasure of the girl's life-force. There is the dual strength of fear and of beauty: the two emotions commingle in this incident. Wordsworth is grateful years later that "feeling comes in aid / Of feeling, and diversity of strength / Attends us, if but once we have been strong" (p. 578).

2

Both Wordsworth's poetry and the debates of the early 1840s con-cerning capital punishment would have been readily available to the young Coventry Patmore when he was working as an assistant librarian in London's British Museum. E. J. Oliver is one of several critics who attests to Patmore's "veneration for Wordsworth."[9] At this point in his career Patmore was 21 years old, financially insecure and uncertain as to his prospects for literary fame. Sister Mary Anthony Weinig, SHCJ, calls the period between January 1845 and July 1846 "the leanest months of Patmore's career"—she explains that "With small fame and smaller funds Patmore played a double role of impecunious poet and harassed reviewer. His father's monetary losses had left the sons, hitherto free enough of severe financial strain, to earn a hand-to-mouth livelihood by their literary talents. In 1845 Coventry appeared regularly in *Douglas Jerrold's Shilling Magazine*."[10] In 1845 he took the bold step of publishing in *Douglas Jerrold's Shilling Magazine* a poem on the topic of public executions entitled "The Murderer's Sacrament: A Fact." Selected portions of this longer poem were included as "A Sketch in the Manner of Hogarth" in his 1853 volume *Tamerton Church-Tower*; an even shorter version called "A London Fête" was published in the 1909 and 1949 editions of Patmore's *Poems*. Patmore appended the following note to the 1853 edition of the poem: "I understand that these verses, which were first printed some years ago, have been regarded as indirectly advocating the abolition of punishment by death. I had no such intention in composing them."

A detailed textual comparison of the several versions of Patmore's poem on the subject of a Victorian public execution would be a useful exercise in textual scholarship. However, there are two relevant points to be stressed here: Patmore's conception of his role as poet and of the general public, and his early use of male-female duality. The mere fact that Patmore shortened his poem each of the three times he successively published it indicates that he had less confidence in the importance of his message. His final version is equal in length to only two or three of Wordsworth's 14 didactic sonnets on the issue. Furthermore, what he saves and what he omits is revealing. As Weinig briefly indicates, the "more factual and less moralizing portions" of the 1845 version are included in the 1853 version."[11] Furthermore, the section of the poem that offers a bitingly negative depiction of the urban crowd at the execution is retained in all three versions:

> Mothers held up their babes to see,
> Who spread their hands, and crow'd for glee;
> . . . .
> A baby strung its doll to a stick;
> A mother praised the pretty trick;

Two children caught and hang'd a cat;
Two friends walk'd on, in lively chat;
And two, who had disputed places,
Went forth to fight, with murderous faces.[12]

In this section of the poem, Patmore—like Dickens, Thackeray, and other Victorian observers—is perturbed by the tendency of public hangings to brutalize the sensibilities of the spectators. Patmore's final version of the poem focuses not on the executed murderer but on the London mob. The crowd witnesses a public display of the imposition of capital punishment, but it has *no* cathartic or deterrent effects. The mob disperses into individual figures (both male and female) who leave the scene one by one to commit violent crimes of their own.

Two latent attitudes are present in this early poem by Patmore: a detestation for democracy and the urban masses and a recognition of the importance to Victorian society of the interplay of masculine and feminine principles (though admittedly distorted in this situation). Unlike Wordsworth, who hoped to use the real language of the common man in his poems and to deal with issues of common human nature, Patmore feels threatened by the common man en masse. As his career developed, he became increasingly authoritarian and anti-democratic. When he depicted crowds of people, he often used animal-cluster metaphors. In an 1887 essay, for example, Patmore used the parable of a sheep's carcass found in a country lane to record his fear that the "ordered state of England" was being transformed into the "pulsating mass of grubs" known as democracy.[13] Other statements of his reactionary politics are well known to Victorian scholars.

Another Patmorean concept latent in this early poem is the principle of sexual duality. As J. C. Reid explains it, "Just as in marriage, man supplies reason, intellectual strength and controlling power, while woman supplies sensitivity, moral force and emotional richness, so in society the feminine element is the masses, governed mainly by emotions."[14] In his poem describing the unruly actions of the crowd at a public execution, Patmore clearly links the riotous and hysterical activity most directly with feminine participants—even more shocking for the fact that they are mothers. In the one line "crow'd for glee" the close approximation of "crowd" and "crow'd" effectively suggests the cacophonous sounds of animal-like screeching. The rational balance of the masculine force is difficult to detect in this poem; however, it seems a likely probability that the "Two friends" who are described as walking on "in a lively chat" represent the masculine powers of reason and logical discussion.

3

In 1868, when A. E. Housman was only nine-years-old, the last public execution in England took place. Executions, however, continued to be carried out privately behind prison walls until capital punishment was outlawed entirely in Great Britain in 1983. The memory of past executions of legendary murderers and the issue of capital punishment continued to be discussed in poems written by such late Victorian and early 20th century poets as A. E. Housman, Thomas Hardy, Oscar Wilde, and Edward Thomas. Of these writers, Housman wrote the most, and the most interesting, poems on the subject.

In the 1890s Housman composed a series of poems that he published in 1896 as *A Shropshire Lad*. Two poems in the volume use scenes of rural memory in the Wordsworthian tradition employed in Book 12 of *The Prelude*; two other poems make general and incompletely defined statements that hangings took place due to quarrels or sacrifices involving love relationships. In Poem IX Housman contrasts the public executions of the past with the private executions of the present. In the past, the hanging body of the murderer served as a harsh presence to warn others against the certain penalties of crime:

> On moonlit heath and lonesome bank
> The sheep beside me graze;
> And yon the gallows used to clank
> Fast by the four cross ways.

> A careless shepherd once would keep
> The flocks by moonlight there,
> And high amongst the glimmering sheep
> The dead man stood on air.[15]

In past days—"A hundred years ago" (p. 22)—the gallows commanded respect and attention. Its location was prominent as it dominated the surrounding landscape and was strategically placed near the intersection of "the four cross ways." Now, however, executions are carried out inside and in private: "They hang us now in Shrewsbury jail" (p. 21). Although Housman expresses his sympathy for the modern victim, he also stresses the deflated stature of the ritual as it is currently practiced. The modern victim of society's justice is like a helpless animal who is caught wriggling in a string. There is no suggestion here of the sacred dimension of the hangman's rope as relic as Michael Jasper traces the tradition in his essay. The rope is now a strangling string that controls a helpless, diminished, and debased puppet:

> And naked to the hangman's noose
> The morning clocks will ring
> A neck God made for other use
> Than strangling in a string. (p. 21)

Poem XLII, "The Merry Guide," also offers a comparison between the sensitivity and "solitude of shepherds" in hamlets near "hanging woods" and the indifference and hectic activities of people in the "far-discovered town" (p. 62). Another well-known poem by Housman—first published in *Last Poems* (1922)—that describes a young man's execution in the town's "market-place" is "Eight O'Clock" (p. 115).

Two poems in *A Shropshire Lad* rely on a muted version of the male-female dichotomy pattern used by such previous poets as Wordsworth and Patmore as well as by many writers of popular broadsides. Again, the link between murder and sex is strong, but Housman gives his own filtered, even allegorical interpretation of the subject. In Poem XVI the disappointments of love—rather than society's justice—drive a whole section of a local cemetery to their graves: "The nettle on the graves of lovers / That hanged themselves for love" (p. 29). In the poem's final quatrain, however, Housman moves from the scene of mass suicides to focus his sympathy on the plight of one unnamed male figure:

> The nettle nods, the wind blows over,
> The man, he does not move,
> The lover of the grave, the lover
> That hanged himself for love. (p. 29)

It is conceivable that the "unmoved lover" may be a reference to Moses Jackson, a college friend for whom Housman felt an intense, but unrequited attraction. Without going into further details here, such a reading of this poem is significant in another respect—that is, that Housman is writing about the subject of self, of self-punishment and denial, in some of the poems about executions. This issue again is relevant to Poem XLVII, "The Carpenter's Son," in which an elaborate allegory involving references to Christ's life is evident. Surely Housman wonders what might be his own fate as a poet who reports the ills of the world to an unsympathetic audience. But by the poem's end he renders his clear opinion: it is better to let the wrongs of the world alone. Before Housman reaches this position, however, he offers a graphic reinactment of history's most famous public execution, the Crucifixion of Jesus Christ:

> "Now, you see, they hang me high
> And the people passing by
> Stop to shake their fists and curse;
> So 'tis come from ill to worse.

> "Here hang I, and right and left
> Two poor fellows hang for theft:
> All the same's the luck we prove,
> Though the midmost hangs for love. (p. 70)

Two other poems in Housman's volume *Last Poems* (1922) that use the motif of hanging to express the problems of self-identity are Poems XII and XIV. In Poem XII he chafes at both "The laws of God, the laws of man" (p. 111). The speaker desires personal independence and endorses rebellion:

> . . . let God and man decree
> Laws for themselves and not for me;
> And if my ways are not as theirs
> Let them mind their own affairs. (p. 111)

The poem is a statement endorsing personal assertion of self and homosexual love. However, the speaker realizes society's powerful threat of conformity and punishment—"With jail and gallows and hell-fire" (p. 111). Likewise, in Poem XIV, "The Culprit," Housman focuses on self and not on social issues. He views his own birth as a form of ultimate punishment that he himself deserves. He absolves his parents from blame or responsibility and concludes that he himself is the real culprit: "And here 'tis only I / Shall hang so high" (p. 114). The "only I" reference becomes fully understandable by the poem's end as Housman concludes that the only way to stop the sufferings of the human experience is to make a conscious choice not to marry or have children:

> For so the game is ended
> That should not have begun.
> My father and my mother
> They had a likely son,
> And I have none. (p. 114)

In these poems and a few others, Housman used the motif of executions to express his private emotions. He framed his own feelings of captivity and social repression in terms of the mechanics of a larger social debate. This is not to say that he did not oppose capital punishment or loathe the details of the suffering that it involved. It is this outlook that connects Housman to a larger 19th century tradition of poets in the "high literary mode." But it is also evident that he represents an endpoint in the poet's own conception of his ability to influence public opinions and issues through his writings. What Gray writes of Housman's poetic identity is by and large true: "His Poems end always in the same perception. The knowing never itself changes or develops, nor does it ever change anything else. His poems say just enough, and say it just often enough, to remind us that the very saying of poetry is an assertion of self and an act of order. But in his view the poem does not, as Housman's high romantic predecessors would have it, alter the conditions and relations of being; it only assists us to endure them."[16] Certainly Wordsworth believed that his sonnets upon the death penalty were intended to alter society's attitude. Patmore's shrill satire missed its mark: he ended up attacking the readers in a democracy and adding footnotes that he supported capital punishment after all. Housman writes on the topic of public and private hangings not for the purpose of wider social reform but for use in depicting his own personal crises.

For those who feel that the distinctions just outlined are "a bit too neat," there is the further puzzle of the fascinating purposes to which several poems by Housman on the issue were put by Clarence Darrow in one of the most famous murder trials of 20th century America, the Loeb and Leopold trial in 1924.[17] Several investigations are in order here because they reveal much about the function of poetry in the 20th century and about the continuing debate concerning capital punishment in American society.

During three hot summer weeks in a Chicago courtroom in 1924, Clarence Darrow, a liberal lawyer and social reformer, defended Nathan Leopold and Richard Loeb in a sensational kidnapping and murder case. Darrow's introduction of psychiatric evidence and his masterly summation — which lasted for two days — saved his clients from the death penalty. Part of his closing argument involved a description of the horrible process of state executions. To assist in painting graphic word pictures, Darrow read several poems on the subject by A. E. Housman, including the recently published "Eight O'Clock." It was an exceptional use of his poetry that would have surprised Housman. In fact, when the two gentlemen actually met in Cambridge three years later to discuss the matter, Housman expressed no pleasure in the famous lawyer's use of his poetry to work good in the wider world, but instead complained that in reading the transcript of the trial given to him by Darrow, several misquotations of his poems are to be condemned. Thus, Housman writes of the visit in a 29 December 1927 letter addressed to his brother Basil: "I had a visit not long ago from Clarence Darrow, the great American barrister for defending murderers. He had only a few days in England, but he could not return home without seeing me, because he had so often used my poems to rescue his clients from the electric chair. Loeb and Leopold owe their life sentence partly to me; and he gave me a copy of his speech, in which, sure enough, two of my pieces are misquoted."[18] That Housman did not share the grand ambition of Wordsworth for seeing his poems on social issues do their work in the world can also be seen in Housman's refusal to allow his poem "Eight O'Clock" to be reprinted in a popular American anthology, *Free Vistas, an Anthology of Life and Letters* (1933). Housman wrote tersely to the editor: "If you do not mind, I would rather that you did not reprint 'Eight o'clock' in your annual. I always give permission rather reluctantly, and there seems to be no particular fitness in its appearance."[19] Clearly by the time of Housman's death in 1936 — 100 years after the initial parliamentary debates on the issue that inspired Wordsworth's sequence of 14 sonnets — the voice of poets for framing the feelings in the debate concerning capital punishment and society-sanctioned executions was a small one. Increasingly, in courtrooms and libraries, poetry gave way to the expert testimony of psychiatrists and sociologists in the 20th century.

Notes

1. See David D. Cooper, *The Lesson of the Scaffold: The Public Execution Controversy in Victorian England* (Athens: Ohio University Press, 1974) and Beth Kalikoff, *Murder and Moral Decay in Victorian Popular Literature* (Ann Arbor, Mich.: UMI Research Press, 1986).

2. Donald J. Gray, "Preface," in *Victorian Literature: Poetry*, ed. Donald J. Gray and G. B. Tennyson (New York: Macmillan, 1976), ix.

3. Donald J. Gray, "William Wordsworth," in *Victorian Literature: Poetry*, ed. Donald J. Gray and G. B. Tennyson (New York: Macmillan, 1976), 3-4.

4. Gray, "William Wordsworth," 4.

5. Sir Henry Taylor, "The Sonnets of William Wordsworth. Collected in One Volume," *Quarterly Review* 69 (December 1841): 1-51.

6. Seraphia D. Leyda, "Wordsworth's *Sonnets Upon the Punishment of Death*," *Wordsworth Circle* 14 (Winter 1983): 48-53.

7. William Wordsworth, *Poetical Works*, ed. Thomas Hutchinson, revised by Ernest de Selincourt (New York: Oxford University Press, 1969), 405. All references to Wordsworth's poetry are to this edition; page numbers will be cited parenthetically.

8. Leyda, "Wordsworth's *Sonnets Upon the Punishment of Death*," 51.

9. E. J. Oliver, *Coventry Patmore* (London: Sheed and Ward, 1956), 33.

10. Sister Mary Anthony Weinig, SHCJ, *Coventry Patmore* (Boston: G. K. Hall, 1981), 50, 47.

11. Ibid., 48.

12. Coventry Patmore, *The Poems of Coventry Patmore*, ed. Frederick Page (New York: Oxford University Press, 1949), 56-57. All references to Patmore's poetry are to this edition; page numbers will be cited parenthetically.

13. Coventry Patmore, *Principle in Art, Etc.*, 2nd ed. (London: George Bell, 1890), 217.

14. J. C. Reid, *The Mind and Art of Coventry Patmore* (London: Routledge and Kegan Paul, 1957), 218.

15. A. E. Housman, *The Collected Poems of A. E. Housman*, ed. John Carter (New York: Holt, Rinehart and Winston, 1965), 21. All references to Housman's poetry are to this edition; page numbers will be cited parenthetically.

16. Donald J. Gray, "A. E. Housman," in *Victorian Literature: Poetry*, ed. Donald J. Gray and G. B. Tennyson (New York: Macmillan, 1976), 829.

17. For a complete discussion of the trial, see Clarence Darrow, *The Story of My Life* (New York: Charles Scribner's Sons, 1932), 226–43, and Kevin Tierney, *Darrow: A Biography* (New York: Thomas Y. Crowell, 1979), 320–51.

18. A. E. Housman, *The Letters of A. E. Housman*, ed. Henry Maas (London: Rupert Hart-Davis, 1971), 257.

19. Ibid., 319.

"Hats Off!": The Roots of Victorian Public Hangings

MICHAEL JASPER

It is a statement that, at first glance, would seem impossible: 19th century England, characterized by an almost paranoid middle- and upper-class fear of the mob and the prudish morality for which the Victorians are known even today, witnessed some of the largest, most violent mobs in English history, and these mobs were formed by the sanction of and, in the case of schoolchildren, the very mandate of, the legal authorities. The mobs I am speaking of were the crowds surrounding public executions. It was common in both England and Scotland for tens of thousands of spectators, from every layer of the social strata, to attend the hangings of notorious murderers. Thirty thousand or more witnessed the executions of James Greenacre in May 1837; the Swiss butler Courvoisier, the killer of Lord William Russell, in 1840; George and Maria Manning in 1849; and Dr. William Palmer, the Rugeley Poisoner, in June 1856. Schools were let out early; parents escorted their children to that Newgate classroom to learn their dire lesson. The gallows was a boogeyman.

Hanging joined the Derby and the Oxford-Cambridge boat race as examples of rare public events at which the classes mixed willingly. Because of their singular life-style, and a poverty that precluded most forms of public entertainment, the poor attended hangings. Shops closed for the day and crowds gathered even before daybreak, braving all sorts of inclement weather, to get a good view. In addition, the condemned was very often one of their own, and great sport was made over whether the prisoner would go bravely to his end. Justin Atholl states that "so long as the hanging was public, the hardened criminal could aspire to no higher epitaph than 'He died game.'"[1]

It would be too easy to explain away riotous crowds as a violent reaction by the disenfranchised and the disillusioned directed against this most deadly display of law and order. "Stuffy they [the upper classes] may have been, but they liked strong meat and were prepared to suffer considerable discomfort for it or pay highly – the fact that seats in windows and housetops sold like hot cakes for guineas in an era when 10s. a week was a not uncommon wage ... suggests that interest was by no means confined to the lower orders."[2] So wealthy Londoners were always a part of these crowds. Both Henry Mayhew and Charles Dickens watched the Mannings hang in 1849, and both wrote of the event. At the execution of Courvoisier, Dickens looked down from his perch in a rented flat above the throng, spied a familiar face, and exclaimed to the members of his party, "Why, there's Thackeray!"

Public hangings were abolished, largely due to official fear of the crowds, in 1868. Beth Kalikoff maintains that the executions themselves had become, for the spectators, "a type of blood sport, [they] re-establish the order that the murder had torn asunder." She also states that "details of crowd size and misbehavior suggest that the appeal of hanging was a sporting one."[3] A hanging, though intended by the authorities as a moral lesson, was a combination of drama, spectacle, sport, and quasi-religious festival. Therefore Kalikoff's analogy, while colorful, is quite accurate. In his *History of Crime in England*, Luke Owen Pike describes a typical 19th century hanging: "men and boys, and even women and girls, repaired to the place of execution to take their pleasure in seeing a fellow human being hanged. The rich and the idle paid high prices for places commanding a good view, as at the theatre, or any other common spectacle. The poor, who loved the excitement as well as their betters, ate cakes and passed ribald jokes from one to another."[4] Pike's reference to the theater is a common theme, one prevalent in the sources of the day. Dickens referred to the theater in his famous letters to the *London Times*, as did Thackeray in his essay "Going to See a Man Hanged," published in *Fraser's Magazine* late in 1840. Thackeray's account is a sociopolitical commentary; its focus is on a larger moral issue. But couched in his purple prose is this short, but provocative scene: "As the clock begins to strike, an immense sway, a movement swept over the whole of that vast dense crowd ... a great murmur arose, more awful, more bizarre, and indescribable than any sound I have ever heard before. Women and children began to shriek horribly."[5]

Thackeray's scene is understandably melodramatic, considering this abolitionist writer's purpose for reporting the incident in the first place. Most, but not all, of the literature "about" public executions is of one of two bents: the sort of propaganda such as that quoted above, or broadside ballads sold as programs for pennies to the assembled crowd. Both acknowledge the existence of a massive audience. While abolitionists wrote about the feral behavior of the mob, the broadsides catered to, and profited from, that same mob. Broadsides, printed and distributed in runs of several thousands, bore the bloody details of the killer's crime beneath a stock drawing of a faceless figure strung on the gibbet. (In the 1849 Mannings broadside, the crude hourglass silhouette of a woman was hurriedly added to the stock figure.)

An 1846 letter to the *Daily News*, written by Dickens in response to Courvoisier's execution, is indicative of a 19th century crowd: "No sorrow, no salutary terror, no abhorrence, no seriousness; nothing but ribaldry, debauchery, levity, drunkenness, and flaunting vice in fifty other shapes . . . I hoped, for an instant, that there was some sense of Death and Eternity in the cry of "Hats off!" when the miserable wretch appeared; but I found, next moment, that they only raised it as they would at a Play—to see the Stage the better, in the final scene."[6] Dickens was also to write to a foreign friend, "The conduct of the people was so indescribably frightful, that I felt . . . as if I were living in a city of devils."[7] This was a typical upper-class reaction—the mob as a quasi-human or even a subhuman gathering—and it was this gut feeling more than any pangs of conscience that led to the 1868 act that forever sent the hangman behind prison walls.

Such accounts as these are obviously stones upon which ideological axes are ground. Yet the litany of mob violence is a long one, and it is doubtful that any other form of social unrest resulted in more deaths than the frightful mob scenes that took place around executions. In 1807, at a triple execution, there was such a press of spectators that "some fell, and others tumbled over them; till there were two or three heaps of persons in this situation, all struggling with each other to extricate themselves."[8] The tally: 30 dead, 15 injured. The previous year, in 1806,[9] another triple hanging resulted in a crash fatal or harmful to over 100 people: "A woman with a child at her breast felt herself being pressed to death and handed the child to the nearest man. He in turn handed it to another and the child was passed from hand to hand over the heads of the mob ... afterwards marshalls and constables cleared the area and found nearly 100 people dead or unconscious."[10] Compare the death toll of this tragedy—between 20 and 40, even assuming the different reports to be of the same riot—to the single death of the now legendary date of November 13, 1887—Bloody Sunday.

The spectators at 19th century hangings were very much participants in the action; but paradoxically, violence most often occurred when the hangman was incompetent, and thus appeared to be deliberately cruel to the condemned criminal. There is something ironic in a crowd, gathered to witness a death, becoming violent in disgust over an unmerciful execution.

On the last day of 1818 a hangman, John Simpson, allowed too much rope in the drop. The prisoner, a robber, still had his toes on the platform and was strangling slowly. A shower of curses and stones followed, and all except the dangling prisoner were forced to retreat from the scaffold. The crowd then cut the unconscious man down: "A riot ensued. [Rioters] smashed windows of the church, stoned the police, and tried unsuccessfully to demolish the scaffold. John Simpson, being in the hands of the rioters, 'suffered severely.'"[11]

Edinburgh's official hangman botched a job in late 1833; he too caused a prisoner to strangle slowly to his death. After the event the hangman was forced into a garden by the vengeful crowd: "They pursued him into the garden ... struck and abused him. [He] ran towards the river, followed by the crowd, who showered stones after him, several of which struck him."[12] This unfortunate "Jack Ketch"[13] was rescued by police after an icy river swim.

Victorian spectators were at once bloodthirsty and jubilant. They exchanged jokes and bottles. When hangman James Botting pulled the trap on the Cato Street conspirators, the ritual of the time was still to behead the traitor, and to display the head to the crowd with the recitation, "This is the head of a traitor." At this hanging Botting held each head up to a rowdy audience that hissed and shouted its dislike for the criminals.[14] But as Botting lifted the last head, it slipped from his fingers and a derisive cry rang out: "Butterfingers!"

Executions were not just entertainments, however. They often took on religious or superstitious significance as well. Relics of the event were saved in the manner of relics of the medieval saints. Many believed that the rope used to hang a criminal was a lucky talisman. In 1828 the rope upon which swung William Corder, the killer of Maria Marten in the Red Barn, sold for a guinea an inch; and two inches of William Palmer's hangman's rope sold for 2/6d. in 1856.[15] Part of the hangman's profits were derived from dealing in these necromantic tokens.

Pieces of and contact with the corpse were supposed to have healing properties. Spectators were known to clamber up the scaffold to rub the recently deceased prisoner's skin, which was supposed to cure everything from warts to consumption. And well into the 1890s a piece of William Corder's tanned skin hung for sale in a leather seller's shop in Oxford Street.[16] Maria Manning wore black satin for her hanging in 1849 and it was decades before the material came back into fashion. It never truly did come back until Victoria wore it on her Diamond Jubilee—in 1897![17]

But the 19th century was not a uniquely callous period. There is a curiosity that is abundantly human, perhaps even archetypal, about the machinations of death,[18] and this morbid fascination is one of the few constants in the human experience, an emotion that crosses nearly all cultural and temporal boundaries. The 19th century system of public hangings and the crowd responses to those hangings have a taproot solidly anchored in past tradition. The 19th century is not an endstop or an anomaly in the bloodlust of its crowds. It is a link in a chain reaching from before the Roman Empire on into modern times and, most probably, beyond.[19]

The Roman legal codes, the *civis iuris*, provided for executions by such diverse methods as stoning, crucifixion, or flinging the condemned off a high crag. But death in combat became the most common practice, under the Empire, when each emperor tried to outdo his predecessor in the ostentation of death and torture. The Roman games *became* the judicial punishment. And while the Romans did not invent capital punishment—in fact, the origin of the Roman combats lay in a *softening* of the Etruscan and Egyptian custom of human sacrifice[20]—the Roman system was the cultural phenomenon of spectacular public justice taken to its nth degree. Where Victorian public hangings were *like* blood sport, Roman executions—gladiatorial combats—*were* blood sport. Those who fought in the amphitheater were "condemned criminals, slaves, ne'er-do-wells, and people of low character."[21]

Juvenal wrote, during the height of the Roman games, when up to 175 days in the year were devoted to the games, that the Roman people desired only two things in life: *panem et circenses*, bread and games.[22] Even the smaller towns had amphitheaters that seated 40,000 or more. And, as in the 19th century, rich and poor alike filled the seats. Cicero writes of the trial of Clodia versus the poet Catullus in which Cicero himself represented Catullus. It was a particularly noteworthy trial, because of the notoriety of Clodia's sexual affairs, for the rich Romans, who never mixed with the lower orders, "except at the games," attended. Apparently, important public events, trials and the like, did not attract the crowds as did the bloody shows at the Colosseum.

The average Roman hungered for the same strong meat as did the average Victorian. This hunger was to some so great that people often died of exposure in the heat of these all-day programs. The average spectacle at the local amphitheater included "horse and chariot races, combats with wild beasts, boxing bouts and dramatic presentations."[23] And, of course, the combats. Often 10,000 men passed through the dust of the circus in a single day in Rome. Boxers' fists were girded with lead, men were bound to posts and ripped by wild beasts. Lucretius, in his *De Rerum Natura*, writes of the scythe-bearing chariots, whose wheels were equipped with blades to sever the arms or head of fallen charioteers. Romans demanded blood for their entertainment. In one of his *Epistles* Horace paints this portrait of Roman live theater: "The people, even while the actors are speaking the verses, call for a bear show or a wrestling match."

There is no real difference between 1st and 19th century crowds. This account of a procession in Rome during Caesar's ascension could easily be a description of Dickensian London: "Past alleys stinking of urine and decaying garbage they walked, dodging lines of clothes hung out to dry by fullers. A wife rubbed a small ball of amber and held it to her nose to dispel the stench."[24]

The crowd was an integral part of the games in Roman society. The crowd decided, by the infamous thumbs up/thumbs down signal, the fate of a fallen gladiator. Judicial pardon amounted to fighting well enough to win the crowd's approval, a notoriously rare occurrence. Death was the heavy toll exacted for incompetence in the ring. Even the winner could be killed at the whim of the crowd for fighting poorly, or for being too merciful to an opponent. A contemporary account of a crowd at the twin cities of Pompeii and Herculaneum is indicative of sports crowds throughout all of history: "Near the close of the race, suspense, anxiety, fury, joy, savagery burst forth. . . . They clapped and shrieked with all their favorites . . . gnashed their teeth, groaned, threatened, exulted, triumphed, and swore."[25] In addition, the 19th century superstitions began in ancient Rome. Romans believed that the blood of a slaughtered gladiator would cure epilepsy. Young *puellae* flocked to the gates of the circus—hair parted with a spear used to kill in combat, they believed, brought good luck in a new marriage.[26]

These "Roman" facets of public executions were common throughout Europe from ancient to Victorian times. Master Franz Schmidt, an executioner in Germany from 1573 until 1617, left behind a detailed journal chronicling his grim profession in which he remarked: "The brutal mobs enjoyed these exhibitions, which frequently gave rise to scenes of coarse revelry and debauch among the onlookers. Drinking and eating booths were set up for the occasion, and the stallholders paid heavy rent to the Council for these pitches. So great were the crowds at times that 200 wagon loads of victuals were found to be barely sufficient to feed the spectators."[27] Schmidt also recorded the demand for relics, physical remains of the dead. Nineteenth century practices in England and Scotland echo his own: "Dead felons were given to the hangman, who sold parts of the corpse very profitably to the superstitious . . . sick people sometimes bribed the *Hochrichter* to allow them to drink the blood streaming from the trunk of the newly beheaded. . . . [People] stole severed heads, or cut off hands, fingers, feet, etc. to sell or use as charms."[28] And, in this same vein: "Many *Hochrichteren* sold at a high price severed hands, human skin, and other ghastly relics valued by the superstitious for the purpose of magic, medicine, or the discovery of hidden treasure."[29]

Schmidt's German crowds held the same appreciation for a job well done as did later Victorian English men and women. They applauded neat workmanship. "Once an artist beheaded two felons with a single stroke, a feat that delighted the onlookers."[30] Schmidt's use of the term "artist" is illuminating. The hangman was a respected figure on the public payroll. A good one commanded quite a salary, a home, plus whatever profits he realized from the sale of relics. As a group, they considered themselves craftsmen, artisans. Bad ones, however, fared no better on the Continent than they did in Great Britain. Schmidt speaks of a hangman who, in 1620, after a cruelly inept execution, at which he needed three strokes to sever the head, "would have been stoned had the crowd been able to loosen the hard frozen clots of earth."[31] Another in 1641 would have come to the same fate, for the same reason, "if the town guard had not come to his help in the nick of time."[32]

Master Franz Schmidt's journal offers a close look at German society in the 16th and 17th centuries, and at the universals of most human societies. For this was also the time of pre-guillotine France, when crowds of thousands flocked around the executioner's platform, his chopping block a great block of ice; of the pillory in England, one step up from stoning, where spectators often killed the prisoner outright with stones and bludgeons; of the first years of the stocks and burning stakes in America.

Public executions, violent and riotous crowds, the demand for and trade in human relics—all were nothing new under the sun. The Victorians were, in fact, in very good company, carrying on traditions started by some of the greatest civilizations of the past. But there is a complexity of crowd responses and social responses to the crowd that is uniquely 19th century England's. British society of the 1800s was particularly fearful of mobs as a social phenomenon. Crowds were a symbol of lower-class disposition and unrest, and the possible changing of the old social guard. So it is not surprising that the act that outlawed public hangings in 1868 was not a bill aimed at prohibiting capital punishment because it was an inhumane practice, but rather a bill aimed at bringing to an end the mobs of lower-class Londoners who gathered for executions.

But even before this law, as well as in the years that followed its passage, Victorian attitudes changed. They grew much wider in scope. They encompassed the entire world, existence itself. When Matthew Arnold spoke of his "ennui," or when James Thomson called his life one of "unattenuated horror," they were not just speaking of their own situation during their own time in their present circumstances. They referred to the outlook of an entire civilization for ages to come. Victorian writers began to see public capital punishments not as a blow to a man's body, or even a man's soul, but as a blow to the soul of a collective humanity. Eventually, as the disillusionment of the age reached full expression, executions were hidden and they lost all symbolic value. This is representative of the Victorian temper from the 1860s on. They turned from social to societal concerns as they began to see how their own age would affect later history.

Notes

1. Justin Atholl, *Shadow of the Gallows* (London: John Long, 1954), 74–75.
2. Ibid., 84.
3. Beth Kalikoff, *Murder and Moral Decay in Victorian Popular Literature* (Ann Arbor: University of Michigan Research Press, 1986), 16.
4. Luke Owen Pike, *A History of Crime in England* (Montclair, N.J.: Patterson Smith, 1968), 2: 451–52.
5. Atholl, *Shadow of the Gallows*, 82.
6. Phillip Collins, *Dickens and Crime* (Cambridge: Cambridge University Institute of Criminology, 1962), 226.
7. Ibid., 240.
8. James Bland, *The Common Hangman: English and Scottish Hangmen Before the Abolition of Public Executions*, ed. H. Snowden Ward (Newton Abbot, England: David and Charles, 1972), 88.
9. Four separate sources—Bland, Potter, Kalikoff, and Atholl—quote three separate dates and as many differing accounts of the number of dead and wounded. There is also confusion as to whether the prisoners were robbers or murderers. On the plain basis of the evidence, there is no reason to doubt the veracity of these sources and to believe that these are separate events. Yet if so, it means that in a little less than a year, between 120 and 150 people were either killed outright or injured in mob-related violence associated exclusively with public hangings. These may be accounts of the same incident, with the details confused or intertwined.
10. Atholl, *Shadow of the Gallows*, 80.
11. Bland, *The Common Hangman*, 117.
12. Ibid., 122–23.
13. "Jack Ketch" was a common nickname given to all hangmen in

Great Britain, derived from the career of the original, who held the position at Newgate from 1678 to 1686, and whose savagery and ineptitude were legendary.

14. Some of the more politically oriented sources indicate cries of remorse and compassion for the prisoners, and disgust at the whole bloody affair. It is hard to reconcile that version with the prevailing portrait of gala crowds and a carnival atmosphere at executions both before and long after this one, but also considering the grisly heckling of this particular crowd directed at the clumsy Botting.

15. John Deane Potter, *The Art of Hanging* (New York: A. S. Barnes, 1965), 70–71.

16. Ibid., 71.

17. Collins, *Dickens and Crime*, 236.

18. Tuttle cites a small number of psychologists whose claim is that the smell of blood enters the primeval structures of the brain, and that this is the cause of violent behavior in the crowds.

19. This statement may seem to be for hyberbolic effect. But as the 1990s approach, one of the most popular selections in any video rental store is a four-part series entitled *Faces of Death*, which purports to show, in graphic detail, the actual deaths of actual people. In addition, news reports describing souvenir-seekers combing scenes of aircraft disasters for bits of flesh and other macabre relics are legion. Indeed, forensic pathology textbooks take this as a matter of course, invariably devoting sections instructing soon-to-be medical examiners on how to work around this problem.

20. Michael Grant, *Gladiators* (New York: Delacorte Press, 1967), 21.

21. Frances Margaret Estes, *Roman Games in the Circus and Amphitheatre* (Columbia: University of South Carolina Press, 1934), 6.

22. All Latin translations are my own.

23. Arthur D. Kahn, *The Education of Julius Caesar: A Biography, A Reconstruction* (New York: Schocken Books, 1986), 124.

24. Kahn, *The Education of Julius Caesar*, 44.

25. Ludwig Friedlander, *Roman Life and Manners under the Early Empire* (New York: Arno Press, 1979), 2: 40.

26. Grant, *Gladiators*, 7.

27. Franz Schmidt, *A Hangman's Diary: The Journal of Master Franz Schmidt*, ed Albrecht Keller, trans. C. W. Calvert and A. W. Gruner (Montclair, N.J.: Patterson Smith, 1973), 62.

28. Ibid., 63.

29. Ibid., 44.

30. Ibid., 55–56. Schmidt also writes with awe of a fellow executioner who was able to sever the head and both hands of a felon with one fell swoop.

31. Ibid., 97.

32. Ibid., 96.

Public Executions in Victorian England: A Reform Adrift

DAVID D. COOPER

The first recorded dissent in Parliament against public executions occurred in 1819, but the real movement to abolish them began in the Victorian period when a group of radicals sought to totally abolish capital punishment. The resulting debate centered on the related matter of public executions and the question of whether it could be demonstrated that they did deter crime. Reformers argued that if capital punishment did not deter crime, it was gratuitously cruel and nonexemplary. Anticapital punishment reformers, as part of their rhetorical assault on the death penalty, condemned public executions as barbarous and grisly, as events that excited criminal passions and hardened people to violence. More moderate reformers wished to retain capital punishment, but hoped to end the practice of public executions. The total abolitionists fought against this idea as tenaciously as their conservative opponents, claiming that advocates of private executions sought merely to prolong capital punishment by hiding its objectionable public example from view.[1]

Also impeding reform of executions was the ingrained belief that the common people would not accept the fact of an execution of a rich, well-connected culprit unless it was performed in public and in open view. If English law was public, as a safeguard against government tyranny, then its punishment must also be public. Belief in this principle was so common that reformers cringed from the suggestion that they sought to tamper with the public infliction of punishment, fearing also condemnation that they advocated private torture. These fears, whether real or contrived, were eroded in time with changing perceptions of government and of the working classes.

Public hangings had a long and fearful history. The practice of taking convicted criminals in procession in open carts to Tyburn had gone on for years until the sheriffs, concerned that the growing disorderliness would detract from the solemnity of punishment, removed executions from Tyburn to Newgate Prison, just outside Debtors' Door. Dr. Johnson complained about the change, grumbling that the object of executions was to draw spectators together and that if they did not draw spectators, "they do not answer their purpose."[2]

Dr. Johnson need not have been concerned, for executions at Newgate proved no less public nor orderly, and just as dangerous to spectators as at Tyburn. A huge crowd packed the spaces before Newgate at the hangings of John Holloway and Owen Haggerty in 1807, and when panic broke out as spectators fought to break free from the crush, nearly 100 persons lay on the street dead or unconscious. A cartload of shoes, hats, petticoats, and other personal items were strewn over the road. The coroner later ruled that the deaths were caused by compression and suffocation.

The penny press with its huge circulation and its method of pandering to its readership with gory, sensationalized details about crime and criminals excited interest in executions.[3] The well-publicized career of Henry Fauntleroy, the banker executed in 1824 as a convicted swindler, brought out swarms of spectators, intrigued by his position in society and by his double life with a succession of mistresses, and also by the persistent rumor of a plot to snatch him from death. A story circulated for many years that Fauntleroy had been revived by surgeons and that he was living on the Continent. Despite the huge audience of witnesses, the belief persisted that a gentleman would not be hanged like a common criminal at the hands of a hangman.

The working classes were not alone in their fascination with crime and criminals. François Courvoisier, convicted for the murder of his master, Lord William Russell, attracted large numbers of persons including lords, ladies, and members of the House of Commons to the service for the condemned at Newgate Chapel, and 600 noblemen and gentlemen were admitted by the sheriff's order into Newgate Prison on the day of his execution on July 6, 1840. William Thackeray was also at the Courvoisier execution; he empathized with the tall, grave

Courvoisier on the scaffold, and felt ashamed and scornful of the entire execution ritual he observed. He was later to write about his trauma and disgust.[4]

No executions in the 19th century, with the exception of the public hanging and decapitation of Arthur Thislewood and his four accomplices of the Cato Street Conspiracy on May 1, 1820, rivaled the executions of the "Five Pirates" in 1864. Despite the spectacular drama of hanging five convicted criminals on the same day, and the huge throng that congregated at Newgate, the executions of the "Five Pirates" were important in themselves as catalysts in galvanizing opposition to public executions.

Crowds swarmed into Newgate on foot, by omnibuses, and by the Metropolitan Underground Railway. Windows in the surrounding houses were filled with expectant faces and people were even clinging to chimney pots on the roofs of nearby buildings. Rented-out upper rooms had been occupied by "swells" who passed the night drinking and playing cards. The public houses, which opened at 5:00 A.M., did a thriving business in the bitterly cold weather. Clerks, pickpockets, prostitutes, roughs, bedraggled women, pinch-faced children—all rubbed shoulders, while vendors hawking chestnuts, oranges, hot potatoes, and greasy pastries moved loudly among them.

As eight o'clock struck, and the Newgate bell began to toll, a sea of faces turned toward the black-draped passage of the Debtors' Door through which the "Pirates" would walk one by one. The first "Pirate" collapsed on the scaffold, a chair was fetched, and he was hanged in that position. The last "Pirate" nodded and laughed, and was cheered loudly. At nine o'clock the sheriffs were summoned to witness the cutting down of the bodies and to be present at the certification by the surgeon that the condemned "could never slay or sin again."[5] At three o'clock the bodies of the "Five Pirates" were placed naked into unmarked graves and covered with pavement blocks.

Often rivaling London hangings in numbers of spectators were the hangings in provincial assize towns. These crowds had a similar cross-section of the morbid, the curious, the criminal, and the sadistic. The country people's zest for executions was just as keen as those in London, and on Monday, market-day, they would throng into the towns. As in London, executions in provincial towns were frought with danger.

Twelve persons, mostly women and children, were trampled to death at an execution in Nottingham in 1844. The mayor remonstrated with Sir James Graham, the home secretary, about the need to change the place of executions. Sir James Graham's reply was succinct and clear: the purpose of executions was the terror of example and no place would be acceptable unless large numbers of persons could assemble near the scaffold.

Charles Dickens, like Thackeray, had gone to the execution of Courvoisier in 1840. Disturbed by the memory of what he had seen there, he later wrote long letters to the *Daily News* describing his detestation of public executions and his rejection of capital punishment. These letters initiated his serious public entry into the controversy over public executions and capital punishment and stirred the public debate more than any previous condemnations. In these letters Dickens urged total abolition of the death penalty on the general principle that society would benefit. There were some ambivalences, however, in Dickens about the depth of his disgust with public executions, which he thought caused a morbid preoccupation with criminals, and an uneasy tension which existed in him about his decision to support the abolition of capital punishment because of his deep-rooted revulsion toward murderers.

The execution of the Mannings in 1849 revived the flagging interest in capital punishment started by Dickens's letters in 1846. As in 1846, Dickens raised the intensity of the debate. But now he wrote the editor of the *London Times* to denounce public executions and not to "discuss the abstract question of *capital punishment.*"[6] In his letter to the *Times* he was willing publicly to advocate private executions, which the abolitionists condemned as "private strangulation," and "secret murder." Now he waged war on public executions, and in return he was singled out by the abolitionists, whom Dickens regarded as obstructionists prepared to accept the fearful influences of public executions rather than jeopardize total abolition, as one of the major obstacles in their crusade. A bitter personal struggle had begun.

Abolitionists were outraged at his apostasy and angered that his support for the abolition of public hangings would sabotage their goal. Dickens was roundly condemned and his intentions impugned at a large meeting of abolitionists in London the day following his last letter in the *Times*. The crowd roared its approval when Charles Gilpin stated emphatically that "they were not laboring to substitute one kind of strangulation for another" and "they would never advocate assassination instead of public execution."[7] "A roaring sea" was Dickens's description of the response his two letters whipped up. He had hoped his letters would produce enough agitation to abolish public executions, but he had no confidence now that any change would be made. "The total abolitionists," he complained, "are utterly reckless and would play the deuce with any such proposition in Parliament."[8]

One of the leading criminal law reformers of the 19th century – and the least well known today – was William Ewart. It was Ewart who kept the issue of capital punishment reform before Parliament and the public. He was responsible for an act in 1824 that discontinued the practice of dissecting executed murderers before exposing the body to public view, and in the same year he sponsored an act that abolished capital punishment for felons who illegally returned after transportation. His most important act gave persons charged with crimes full protection of legal counsel. The zenith of abolitionist hopes was reached on March 5, 1840, when Ewart rose in the House of Commons to make an historic resolution to abolish capital punishment entirely (by 1840 execution was by practice only for murder). Inevitably, the related matter of public executions was brought into the debate, as Ewart sought to show that if public executions did not deter crime with their terrifying gallows scenes, then obviously capital punishment did not deter murderers. Ewart's motion for the abolition of capital punishment reached a high mark with 90 members of the House of Commons voting in support. But the euphoria that followed this vote was premature. The indefatigable Ewart introduced bills to abolish capital punishment in 1849, 1850, 1856, 1864, and 1868, with no success.

Paradoxically, the lesser reform, the abolition of public executions, had virtually no support in 1840. Henry Rich introduced the first motion in the House of Commons to abolish public executions on February 16, 1841, almost a year after Ewart's motion to abolish capital punishment. Although Rich assured the House that executions would be conducted before appropriate witnesses and the press, his motion was totally rejected. Only the member who seconded Rich's motion supported him. Another member astutely observed that Rich had against him not only those in favor of continuing public executions, but also those who were entirely opposed to executions. Rich withdrew his motion. It was such a devastating rejection, that not until 1856, after an interval of 15 years, was the question of the abolition of public execution raised again.

The bishop of Oxford had mixed motives when he raised the issue of abolition in the House of Lords in 1856. On the one hand, he repeated the familiar arguments about the great evils that had risen from the system of public executions, but on the other hand he feared capital punishment would be resisted unless the method of execution was changed. He was particularly alarmed that women were escaping punishment, even for the "highest offenses,"[9] because of increased reluctance to carry out the ultimate sentence of the law. He recommended to his peers the American system of executing criminals before witnesses as an alternate model.

As a result of the bishop of Oxford's initiative the Select Committee on Capital Punishment of the House of Lords, with the bishop as chairman, was created to look into public executions. A recurring fear expressed before the Select Committee was the concern that the public would not accept that the death sentence would be inflicted if the criminal were educated or well-to-do. Lord Lansdowne recalled that as a schoolboy he repeatedly heard the rumor that the Reverend Dr. Dodd, a well-known minister, had been seen walking the streets of London 10 to 20 years after his execution.[10] The testimony given to the Select Committee continually expressed concern that care must be taken to assuage such deep-rooted suspicion. Even private executions performed before competent witnesses were not sufficient assurance for one witness who recommended that the victim's body must be exhibited before the prison as conclusive proof. Testimony touching on the American method of private executions aroused intense interest, and J. P. Kennedy, formerly secretary of the navy in President Fillmore's cabinet, was questioned at greater length than any other witness. Kennedy assured the lords that the private executions already introduced in many American states were so successful that this method would soon be employed in every state.

The Select Committee of the House of Lords on Capital Punishment reported that public executions had no deterring effect, and that the system of executions glorified the criminal, cast him in a martyr's role, and lightened the terrors of death. The committee report recommended that henceforth executions should take place within prison walls, noting that other countries including Prussia and the United States executed criminals within prison walls without injurious consequences and with the approval of strong public opinion.

Both radical and conservative opinion condemned the report. Henry Mayhew warned that giving the government the right to put men to death secretly would lead to secret trials and to the "times of the Old Bastille."[11] The *Times*, expressing conservative opinion, accused the Select Committee of seeking to undermine the cherished English system of government by doing away with publicity, one of the cherished bulwarks of English freedom.

Despite the support of a committee of the House of Lords, the hope of ending public hangings remained remote. Antagonism against change by the press, the lord chief justice, and the home secretary produced an opposition of irresistible force. Although the movement for reform in 1856 was dim, another step had been taken, and private executions had been sanctioned by an authoritative committee of the House of Lords.

Following the controversy over the executions of the "Five Pirates" in 1864, William Ewart's efforts to abolish the death penalty led to the formation of the Royal Commission on Capital Punishment. Before this distinguished body the principle of publicity so long maintained by succeeding governments was finally breached. Spencer Walpole, home secretary in 1852 and 1858, and Sir George Grey, the current home secretary, gave jarring dissents to the long-held belief that the terror of public executions acted as a deterrent to the commission of crime. Walpole now questioned this belief so long sanctified by time and practice, believing, instead, that public executions encouraged crime. Sir George Grey was profoundly influenced by accounts of private executions in America and Australia without any of the ill-effects predicted so often by opponents of private executions.

The majority of the members of the Royal Commission determined from the evidence given them "a preponderance of opinion" against public executions. They issued the "Report of the Capital Punishment Committee" on January 8, 1866, which recommended that executions should be carried out within the precincts of the prison under such regulations as may be considered necessary to prevent abuses and to satisfy the public that the law had been complied with. The four abolitionists on the Royal Commission substituted a minority report that urged the abolition of capital punishment "at once."

Gathorne Hardy, who had been a member of the Royal Commission and who had become home secretary, introduced the Capital Punishment within the Prisons Bill on November 26, 1867. The new home secretary was emphatic about not considering any measure relating to reform of the criminal law except the matter of public executions, condemning them as a species of amusement that no longer had a desirable effect on the criminal classes. He reassured the House of Commons that private executions were effective deterrents that would suppress the murderous instincts of the criminal classes by a more fearful, awe-inspiring, silent death.

Charles Gilpin, an outspoken abolitionist, objected: "if hanging be acknowledged to be so unclean a thing that it is no longer to be tolerated in the broad sunlight"[12] the English people will have none of it. He moved to amend the bill to make executions private read that capital punishment be abolished instead. But even John Stuart Mill had to announce that he could not support the abolition of capital punishment. The crusade to abolish capital punishment had come to an end, not to be seriously resurrected again until the 20th century. The weaknesses of all the arguments used against private executions were exposed by the ease with which the Capital Punishment within the Prisons Bill passed through the House of Lords.

While the legislation was moving through Parliament, parts of England appeared under siege by Fenian terrorism. The Fenians, a secret society formed in 1858, did not take up arms in earnest in the struggle for Irish independence until the American Civil War ended, and a number of battle-hardened Irish veterans returned to swell its ranks. After an aborted uprising in Ireland in March, 1867, the struggle shifted to England, where in an attempt to rescue Fenian prisoners a Manchester constable was killed. Three young Irishmen who had taken part in the raid were arrested. Though none of them was proved to have fired the fatal shot, they were convicted of the murder, and the execution date was set for November 23, 1867.

Working-class and radical support for the convicted Fenians was soon mobilized. Protest meetings against the forthcoming executions spread throughout England. Organized committees of working-class men protesting the hangings sprang up in different cities. Despite the deputation of working men sent to urge the home secretary to commute the death sentences, the executions of the "Manchester Martyrs" — as Irish circles were to refer to them — were carried out under the most stringent security. Anticipating violent protest and fearing rescue attempts, the government deployed an artillery detachment, troops of the 72nd Highlanders, and 2,500 special constables. The *Times* stated that the executions of the Fenians had excited more public interest than any other previous executions in living memory.

Overnight their executions turned the previously unknown men into national martyrs. Huge protest demonstrations were held in Ireland and England. Tensions and rumors concerning Fenian insurrectionary activities continued for a month after the executions.

Events caused by the attempt to free Richard Burke from Clerkenwell Prison precipitated intense fears of Fenian terrorism and insurrection that almost bordered on paranoia. Burke, considered by Gathorne Hardy as the leading Fenian "at the bottom of the bad conspiracies,"[13] became the focus of a plot to free him and Joseph Casey, a fellow Fenian, from Clerkenwell Prison. The plot was a simple one: a barrel of gunpowder placed next to the outside wall of the prison would blow a hole through it between three and four o'clock during the exercise period when Burke and Casey would be in the prison courtyard with other prisoners.

On December 14, 1867, a blast almost ripped away the solid wall of the prison. The houses on Corporation Row, a narrow lane fronting the northern side of the prison, suffered the most damage. One of the houses was reduced to a heap of debris, and others were wrecked as though shattered by earthquake and ravaged by fire. Twelve persons were killed and 120 were wounded, some very seriously.[14] A wave of sympathy for the victims was the immediate response to the Clerkenwell explosion — soon termed the "Clerkenwell Outrage." Fenians were now characterized as reckless criminals. The working-class press, which had previously been sympathetic to the executed Manchester Fenians, now denounced the Clerkenwell violence as a "diabolical outrage" and "an act of ferocious wickedness."[15] Irish groups divorced themselves from the Clerkenwell explosion. The London Committee of the Irish Republican Brotherhood pledged to discover and punish those responsible.

The Clerkenwell affair triggered an ever-widening anxiety about real and imagined Fenian disorders, plots, assassinations, and attacks. London and the provinces braced for Fenian violence as rumors and threats spread. Police and the military were dispatched to nearly every part of metropolitan London. Protective forces were thrown around gas factories and powder magazines located in Dartford, Faversham, and Hounslow, and quite unaccountably around the British Museum. Working-class men responded to the call from authorities to become special constables. Scores of workingmen volunteered as special constables in Southward, and a large number of workmen ringed the Chatham Dock to forestall threatened Fenian sabotage there. England took on a siege-like atmosphere as thousands of men received warrants, staves, and special instructions about how to deal with Fenian marauders.

The police and Home Office were also buffeted by threats and rumors. Disraeli informed the cabinet about a projected Fenian attack on the Bank of England, while Gathorne Hardy reported General Grey's concern for the security of Queen Victoria. Hardy added, "and no wonder – for threats are rife and men are ready to execute them."[16] The information which poured into the Home Office was all depressingly the same, Gathorne Hardy complained.

The cataclysmic events that convulsed England appeared not to deter both Houses from abolishing public executions. In the spring of 1868, a Fenian, in reprisal for the hanging of the three Fenians in Manchester, shot the duke of Edinburgh during his Australian tour, and in Canada in April Darcy McGee, a leading Irish-Canadian statesman, was assassinated by a Fenian. Even widespread apprehension over a rash of recent murders in Bristol, Dover, Durham, Todmorden, and London – "a mania for murder" the *Morning Herald* declared – did not undermine the resolve of Parliament to end public executions.

A crime wave, threatened and real violence, a sensational assassination, and another attempted one did not harden a resolve in Parliament to crush murders and check violence with exemplary and brutal lessons of the public gallows. By now even an attempted assassination of royalty could not resurrect the old faith in the deterrent quality of public executions. The dependence on them had passed. Even the *Times* capitulated. It accepted the inevitability and the desirability of private executions, hoping they could put an end to the abhorrent scenes incident to the infliction of capital punishment. Capital punishment would continue, as almost everyone thought it should, but it would now take place in private.

Just three days before the Capital Punishment within the Prisons Bill received the Royal Assent on May 29, 1868, Michael Barrett was hanged, the last person publicly executed in England. Barrett had been convicted of murder as the person who ignited the barrel of gunpowder that exploded the Clerkenwell Prison wall, although seven others had also been apprehended and charged with murder. As the trial progressed before Lord Chief Justice Cockburn and Mr. Bramwell in a special session of the Criminal Court, the testimony weighed heavily against Barrett. The evidence hinged upon the testimony of Patrick Mullany, who had become a witness for the Crown against his former associates. Mullany maintained that Barrett, whom he alleged to have known under the alias of Jackson, had traveled from Glasgow to London purposely to free Burke and that Barrett had admitted to him that he had ignited the barrel of gunpowder. Mullany, who received money from the police after becoming an informer, and who also sought part of the offered reward, gave information placing Barrett in London just before the explosion. Mullany was not the only prosecution witness who was interested in a reward.

Some very contradictory evidence was given against Barrett. A dairyman had positively identified Barrett as the man who had fired the fuse, but when he was called to identify Barrett, he picked out another man who had been arrested with Barrett on a different charge. He explained away his error by admitting he had seen only the side of Barrett's face. Another witness who had positively identified Barrett in the vicinity of Clerkenwell Prison, when pressed, could not swear he was the same man. There was considerable confusion about the clothing Barrett was alleged to have worn, about the type of sideburns he had then, and whether he had whiskers or not.

The chief defense witness was Peter M'Corrie, editor and proprietor of the *Irish Catholic Banner*. He testified that Barrett had attended a meeting in Glasgow on the day Mullany claimed he had spoken to Barrett. The defense produced six other witnesses to corroborate Barrett's claim that he had been in Glasgow during the Clerkenwell explosion. The prosecution strongly implied that Barrett's witnesses had Fenian sympathies, and that their sole reason for testifying was to secure the release of a Fenian. The attorney general tried to identify M'Corrie as a Fenian sympathizer by introducing as evidence articles in the *Irish Catholic Banner* about the three executed Manchester Fenians, called in one issue "our murdered Brethren," and in another "three Irishmen hanged not for murder, but for vindictive feeling."[17]

The lord chief justice's charge to the jury indicated that it must choose between the credibility of Barrett and his Irish witnesses and Mullany and the corroborating evidence of Jane Koepple and Henry Morris, Mullany's employee and apprentice. His instructions to the jury left little doubt that it should deal with the statements placing Barrett in Glasgow during the Clerkenwell explosion as evidence manufactured to save him. His bias against M'Corrie was hardly disguised: "Certainly the sentiments expressed in the columns the editor and publisher of which had been examined were so outrageous and abominable that they amounted to perversion of moral sentiment."[18] The jury found Michael Barrett guilty of murder, but his codefendants were acquitted. Barrett, who had made a considerable impression on the press, asked to address the court before the sentence was read. After a remarkably incisive review of the evidence given against him, he concluded, in part, that "an Irishman's oath will no longer be admitted into a court of justice where the life of a fellow creature is at stake."[19]

Michael Barrett's execution scheduled for May 12, 1868, was postponed twice by Gathorne Hardy to have inquiries made in Glasgow concerning Barrett's alibi. In response to a deputation led by John Bright, Gathorne Hardy acknowledged the need for a continued inquiry, and he sent one of the prosecutors in the case to Glasgow to examine a number of witnesses. The *Morning Advertiser* was doubtful of Barrett's guilt as a result of the new evidence. "If the evidence in support of the alibi, and which this affidavit of the printer Lindsay is an important addition is true," the *Morning Advertiser* declared, "then it would inevitably follow that Michael Barrett cannot be the same person as Jackson"[20] – and the Crown's conviction of Barrett rested on the fact that they were one and the same individual.

The new evidence gathered by the prosecutor and Barrett's counsel and solicitor was referred to the same lord chief justice who had tried the case and who had shown such a strong bias against Barrett's witnesses. Now he was asked to find grounds on which to reverse the verdict. He refused to do so. Despite Bright's request in the House of Commons for the need for a second trial – he thought the conviction of Barrett was not sustained by the evidence – Michael Barrett was executed in front of Newgate Prison on May 26, 1868.[21]

By all the news accounts, the behavior of the crowd was comparatively good. The *Morning Star* thought the crowd quite docile: "It was a crowd that might have been waiting for a coronation, Lord Mayor's show or any public procession."[22] The *Times* thought there was very little to distinguish the last execution from others that preceded it except the crowd was possibly better behaved.[23] During the night before the execution there were very few lights in the windows opposite Newgate and no sounds from the rooms where on previous occasions wealthy revellers made a night of it with drinking and feasting. Down below, among the crowds, there were fewer cries of distress, less maltreatment and robbery than usual.

The muscular, prepossessing Barrett mounted the steps of the scaffold with firmness. A burst of cheers was immediately followed by hisses, but he paid no attention to either. He was very attentive to what the priest was saying to him, and then he began to pray fervently. The executioner put a cap over Barrett's face, adjusted the rope around his neck, the bolt was drawn, and the drop fell with a loud boom and echo.

The newspapers breathed a sigh of relief that Barrett's was the last public execution. The *Daily News* commented that the event demonstrated the expediency of the recent change in the law. It described the crowd at Barrett's hanging as an incarnation of evil persons with perverted sympathies who were unable to show either pity for the criminal or horror for his crime: "The bastard pride in his animal courage and the brutal delight that he died game made the law and its ministers seem to them to be the real murderers, and Barrett to be a martyred man."[24]

The *Times* believed that no one could look on the scene of Barrett's hanging even with all its exceptional quietness, without gratitude that this was the last public execution. "The sight of public executions to those who have to witness them," the *Times* reporter wrote, indicating his own sense of relief "is as disgusting as it must be demoralizing, even to all the hordes of thieves and prostitutes it draws together."[25]

The apprehensions and indecison that had impeded the reform of public hangings were cast aside once concrete information was forth-coming that private executions in the United States and Australia did not arouse the suspicions of the people, but in fact did away with the hideous spectacles of the past.

The new decade of the 1860s had brought with it new conditions and such a change in the moral attitudes and conduct of the lower classes—one social historian described this change as a giant step "towards the humanization of a class of persons who had traditionally been regarded as almost of another species"—that this resulted in a less morbid dread of the "criminal classes."[26] The reduction in crime dur-ing the course of the century—corroborated by recent scholarship[27]—and the new moral tone evident in the country combined to create an awareness that public executions had become a growing source of em-barrassment and an anachronism. William Ewart and his abolitionist supporters had opposed private executions because they thought the continuance of public executions would finally, as a reaction, end capital punishment entirely. Paradoxically, the abolitionists' agitation against capital punishment kept the issue of public executions alive, and it was the end of public executions that Parliament and the public were ready to accept, and not the end of the death penalty. The aboli-tion of public executions was one of a group of reforms enacted in the later 19th century by which time people had grown to abhor brutality in punishments.

Notes

1. That England had not abolished public executions until 1868 I first attributed to reactionaries with a class bias and fear of the working classes. Further reflection and research indicate, rather compellingly, that attempts

to abolish public executions in Parliament had been frustrated for over a quarter of a century by radicals. For a study of public executions in Victorian England and the political maneuvering at reform attempts, see David D. Cooper, *The Lesson of the Scaffold: The Public Execution Controversy in Victorian England* (London: Allen Lane, 1974).

2. Horace W. Bleackley, *The Hangman of England* (London: Chapman and Hall, 1939), 80.

3. The Catnach Press, a prime example of the penny press, was a leading printer of sensational accounts of scandals, murders, and robberies for a growing circulation after the mid-19th century as literacy increased. The Catnach Press was reputed to have sold 2,500,000 broadsides of the Mannings' executions (Charles Hindley, *The History of the Catnach Press* [London: C. Hindley the Younger, 1886], 65-68).

4. Thackeray wrote a bitter article for *Fraser's Magazine* chiding people who paid for places overlooking the scaffold to view a government agent strangling a victim; see his "Going to See a Man Hanged."

5. *Morning Herald*, 23 February 1864. The press generally denounced the executions as another amusement without solemnity or impact.

6. *Times*, 14 November 1849. Dickens had arrived at the conclusion that the abolition of capital punishment would never be accepted in England. The right course for abolitionists, he believed, was to rid the nation of the public gallows. See Walter Dexter, ed., *The Letters of Charles Dickens, 1845-1847* (London: Nonesuch Press, 1938), 2: 185.

7. *Times*, 14 November 1849. Charles Gilpin became so prominent in abolition that the *Eclectic Press* called him "the Cobden of the Abolition Movement" (Vol. 88 [1848], 148).

8. Dexter, *Letters of Charles Dickens*, 2: 186.

9. Debate raged in Parliament and in newspaper editorials in 1856 about the growing problems of infanticide, and the reluctance to hang women. It was the well-publicized murder of a ten-year-old by her stepmother whose death sentence was commuted that caused the bishop of Oxford to take up the issue in the House of Lords concerning women spared from the gallows, which he attributed to a feeling of indecency to execute women in public; see *Hansard*, vol. 142 (1856), cols. 349-50.

10. The Reverend Dr. William Dodd was executed at Tyburn in 1777 for forgery. There was a long-lived rumor that Dodd had a silver tube placed in his throat by the bribed executioner and rushed to Goodge Street to an undertaker where two surgeons revived him.

11. Henry Mayhew, "On Capital Punishment," in *Three Papers on Capital Punishment* (London: Society for the Amendment of the Law, 1856), 63.

12. *Hansard*, Vol. 190 (1868), col. 1136.

13. A.E. Gathorne-Hardy, ed., *Gathorne Hardy, First Earl of Cranbrook: A Memoir* (London: Longman and Co., 1910), 1: 238.

14. Leon O'Broin, *Fenian Fever: An American Dilemma* (New York: New York University Press, 1971), 210.

15. *Beehive*, 21 December 1867.

16. *Lord Cranbrook's Private Diary*, Ipswich and East Suffolk Record Office, 1866-1870, 187.

17. *Times*, 28 April 1868.

18. Ibid.

19. Ibid.

20. *Morning Advertiser*, 8 May 1868.

21. The question whether the police allowed the Clerkenwell explosion to discredit the Fenians occurs. Even Lord Derby, the prime minister, was nonplused, given the sufficient warning about the time, place, and method of blowing up the wall, and "in broad daylight" (see Gathorne Hardy, *A Memoir*, 221–22). Perhaps the most suspicious, and intriguing is no news. The following is stated in the catalog of the Metropolitan Police Records: "Steps taken with reference to threatened rescue of Burke (missing)," Public Record Office HO45 #7799/297.

22. *Morning Star*, 27 May 1868.

23. *Times*, 27 May 1868.

24. *Daily News*, 27 May 1868.

25. *Times*, 27 May 1868.

26. Steven Marcus, *The Other Victorians* (New York: Bantam Books, 1967), 147.

27. Recent scholarship minimizes contemporary accounts of a criminal, working-class population, which finds that the bulk of the crimes committed were neither violent nor organized, but petty forms of thievery and misdemeanors. See the following: David Philips, *Crime and Authority in Victorian England: The Black Country, 1835–1836* (Totowa, N.J.: Rowman and Littlefield, 1977); George Rudé, *Criminal and Victim: Crime and Society in Early Nineteenth-Century England* (New York: Oxford University Press, 1985); Clive Emsley, *Crime and Society in England, 1750–1900* (New York: Longman, 1987); and David Jones, *Crime, Protest, Community in Nineteenth-Century Britain* (London: Routledge and Kegan Paul, 1982). The latter contends that rural crime was more vicious and organized than the crime of the "dangerous criminal classes" congregated in the populated manufacturing districts.

Selected Bibliography

Primary Sources

Analysis and Review of the Blue Book of the Royal Commission on Capital Punishment. London: Society for the Abolition of Capital Punishment, 1866.

Beccaria, Cesare Bonesana. *An Essay on Crimes and Punishments.* (First published in London in 1770; tr. Edward D. Ingraham.) Philadelphia: Philip H. Nicklin, 1819.

Beedle, Susannah. *An Essay on the Advisability of Total Abolition of Capital Punishment.* London: Nichols and Son, 1867.

Beggs, Thomas. *The Royal Commission and the Punishment of Death.* London: Society for the Abolition of Capital Punishment, 1866.

Bovee, Marvin H. *Christ and the Gallows: Or, Reasons for the Abolition of Capital Punishment.* New York: Masonic Publishing Co., 1870.

Dickens, Charles. *Miscellaneous Papers.* 2 vols. Edited by Bertram Waldron Matz. London: Chapman and Hall, 1908.

Dymond, Alfred H. *The Law on Trial, or Personal Recollections of the Death Penalty and Its Opponents.* London: Society for the Abolition of Capital Punishment, 1865. *Three Papers on Capital Punishment.* London: Society for Promoting the Amendment of the Law, 1856.

Evans, Edward Payson. *The Criminal Prosecution and Capital Punishment of Animals.* London: W. Heinemann, 1906.

Fielding, Henry. *An Enquiry into the Causes of the Late Increase of Robbers, with Some Proposals for Remedying This Growing Evil.* London, 1751.

Hanging Not Punishment Enough for Murtherers, Highway Men and House Breakers, Offer'd to the Consideration of the Two Houses of Parliament. London, 1701.

Hill, Frederic. *The Substitute for Capital Punishment.* London: Society for the Abolition of Capital Punishment, 1866.

Hogarth, Georgina, ed. *The Letters of Charles Dickens, 1833–1870.* 3 vols. London: Chapman and Hall, 1909.

Holyoake, George Jacob. *Public Lessons of the Hangman*. London: Farrah, 1864.

Mayhew, Henry, and John Binny. *The Criminal Prisons of London and Scenes of Prison Life*. London: Griffin, Bohn, 1862. *Three Papers on Capital Punishment*. London: Society for Promoting the Amendment of the Law, 1856.

Montagu, Basil. *The Opinions of Different Authors Upon the Punishment of Death*. 3 vols. London: Longman, 1809.

Peggs, James. *Capital Punishment: The Importance of Its Abolition*. London, 1839.

Phillips, Charles. *Vacation Thoughts on Capital Punishment*. London: Cash, 1856.

Quinby, George Washington. *The Gallows, the Prison, and the Poor-House. A Plea for Humanity; Showing the Demands of Christianity in Behalf of the Criminal and Perishing Classes*. Cincinnati: G. W. Quinby, 1856.

Ray, Gordon N., ed. *The Letters and Private Papers of William Makepeace Thackeray*. 4 vols. London: Oxford University Press, 1945–46.

The Royal Commission and the Punishment of Death. London: Society for the Abolition of Capital Punishment, 1866.

Tancred, Sir Thomas. *Suggestions on the Treatment and Disposal of Criminals*. London: T. Hatchard, 1857.

Taylor, John Sydney. *A Comparative View of the Punishments Annexed to Crime in the United States of America, and in England*. London: Harvey and Darton, 1831.

Wakefield, Edward Gibbon. *Facts Relating to the Punishment of Death in the Metropolis*. London, 1832.

Webster, Edward. *Three Papers on Capital Punishment*. London: Society for Promoting the Amendment of the Law, 1856.

The Trial of Charles I: A Documentary History, edited by David Lagomarsino and Charles T. Wood. Hanover, N.H.: University Press of New England, 1990.

Woolrych, Humphrey William. *On the Report of the Capital Punishment Commission of 1866*. London: Society for the Abolition of Capital Punishment, 1866.

Secondary Sources

Babington, Anthony. *For the Sake of Example: Capital Courts-Martial 1914–20*. London: Leo Cooper/Secker & Warburg; New York: St. Martin's Press, 1983.

Bailey, Lloyd R. *Capital Punishment: What The Bible Says*. Nashville, Tenn.: Abingdon Press, 1987.

Baker, William H. *On Capital Punishment*. Chicago: Moody Press, 1985.

Bar, Carl Ludwig von. *A History of Continental Criminal Law.* Boston: Little, Brown, 1916.

Bedau, Hugo Adam. *Death Is Different: Studies in the Morality, Law, and Politics of Capital Punishment.* Boston: Northeastern University Press, 1987.

Berns, Walter Fred. *For Capital Punishment: Crime and the Morality of the Death Penalty.* New York: Basic Books, 1979.

Berry, James. *My Experiences as an Executioner.* Edited by H. Snowden Ward. Newton Abbot, England: David and Charles, 1972.

Bishop, George Victor. *Executions: The Legal Ways of Death.* Los Angeles: Sherbourne Press, 1965.

Black, Charles Lund, Jr. *Capital Punishment: The Inevitability of Caprice and Mistake.* 2d ed. New York: Norton, 1981.

Bland, James. *The Common Hangman: English and Scottish Hangmen before the Abolition of Public Executions.* Hornchurch, Essex, England: I. Henry Publications, 1984.

Bleackley, Horace William. *The Hangmen of England; How They Hanged and Whom They Hanged: The Life Story of "Jack Ketch" Through Two Centuries.* London: Chapman & Hall, 1929.

————. *Some Distinguished Victims of the Scaffold.* London: Kegan Paul, 1905.

————, and John Lofland. *State Executions, Viewed Historically and Sociologically.* Montclair, N.J.: Patterson Smith, 1977.

Block, Eugene B. *When Men Play God: The Case Against Capital Punishment.* San Francisco, Calif.: Cragmont Publications, 1981.

Blom-Cooper, Louis, ed. *The Law as Literature.* London: Bodley Head, 1961.

Bowers, William J., with Glenn L. Pierce and John F. McDevitt. *Legal Homicide: Death as Punishment in America, 1864–1982.* Boston: Northeastern University Press, 1984.

Boyle, Thomas. *Black Swine in the Sewers of Hampstead: Beneath the Surface of Victorian Sensationalism.* London: Hodder; New York: Viking, 1990.

Bye, Raymond Taylor. *Capital Punishment in the United States.* Philadelphia: Committee on Philanthropic Labor of Philadelphia Yearly Meeting of Friends, 1919.

Calvert, Roy. *Capital Punishment in the Twentieth Century.* New York: Putnam, 1936.

————. *Executions.* London: National Council for the Abolition of the Death Penalty, 1926.

Christoph, James Bernard. *Capital Punishment and British Politics; The British Movement to Abolish the Death Penalty, 1945–1957.* Chicago: University of Chicago Press, 1962.

Cohen, Bernard Lande. *Law Without Order: Capital Punishment and the Liberals.* New Rochelle, N.Y.: Arlington House, 1970.

Coit, Stanton. *Public Opinion and the Death Penalty.* London: Edgar G. Dunstan, 1937.

Collins, Philip. *Dickens and Crime.* New York: Macmillan, 1962.

Cooper, David D. *The Lesson of the Scaffold: The Public Execution Controversy in Victorian England.* Athens: Ohio Univ. Press; London: Allen Lane, 1974.

Cornish, W. R., and B. de N. Clark. *Law and Society in England, 1750-1950.* London: Sweet and Maxwell, 1989.

Cox, J. Stevens. "The Dreadful Murder at Stoke Abbott and the Public Execution of James Seale." *Thomas Hardy Yearbook* 1 (1970): 85-93.

Crapo, Paul. "Bryant on Slavery, Copyright, and Capital Punishment." *ESQ: A Journal of the American Renaissance* 47 (1967): 139-40.

Cunningham, Karen. "Renaissance Execution and Marlovian Elocution: The Drama of Death." *PMLA* 105 (March 1990): 209-22.

Davies, James A. "John Forster at the Mannings' Execution." *Dickensian* 67 (1971): 12-15.

Dillon, Richard G. "Capital Punishment in Egalitarian Society: The Meta' Case." *Journal of Anthropological Research* 36 (Winter 1980): 437-52.

Duff, Charles. *A Handbook on Hanging: Being a Short Introduction to the Fine Art of Execution.* London: Journeyman Press, 1981.

Elliott, Robert Greene. *Agent of Death: The Memoirs of an Executioner.* New York: Dutton, 1940.

Foucault, Michel. *Discipline and Punish: The Birth of the Prison.* Translated by Alan Sheridan. New York: Random House, 1979.

Gorecki, Jan. *Capital Punishment: Criminal Law and Social Evolution.* New York: Columbia University Press, 1983.

Groves, David. "DeQuincey's 'Daughter of Lebanon' and the Execution of Mary McKinnon." *Wordsworth Circle* 19 (Spring 1988): 105-7.

Harris, Ruth. *Murders and Madness: Medicine, Law, and Society in the "Fin de Siecle."* Oxford, England: Clarendon Press, 1989.

Harris, Tim. *London Crowds in the Reign of Charles II: Propaganda and Politics from the Restoration until the Exclusion Crisis.* Cambridge: Cambridge University Press, 1987.

Hay, Douglas, and Francis G. Snyder. *Policing and Prosecution in Britain, 1750-1850.* London: Oxford University Press, 1989.

Heline, Theodore. *Capital Punishment: Historical Trends Toward Its Abolishment.* La Canada, Calif.: New Age Press, 1965.

Henry, Patrick. "Camus on Capital Punishment." *Midwest Quarterly: A Journal of Contemporary Thought* 16 (1975): 362-70.

Hood, Roger. *The Death Penalty: A World-Wide Perspective*. New York: Oxford University Press, 1935.

Hooper, William Eden. *The History of Newgate and the Old Bailey*. London: Underwood Press, 1935.

Kalikoff, Beth. *Murder and Moral Decay in Victorian Popular Literature*. Ann Arbor, Mich.: UMI Research Press, 1986.

Koestler, Arthur. *Reflections on Hanging*. London: Gollancz, 1956.

Laurence, John. *A History of Capital Punishment*. New York: Citadel Press, 1960.

Lethbridge, J. P. *Murder in the Midlands*. London: Robert Hale, 1989.

Levy, Barbara. *Legacy of Death*. Englewood Cliffs, N.J.: Prentice-Hall, 1973.

Leyda, Seraphia D. "Wordsworth's *Sonnets Upon the Punishment of Death*." *Wordsworth Circle* 14 (Winter 1983): 48–53.

Mackey, Phillip. *Hanging in the Balance*. New York: Garland, 1982.

Maestro, Marcello T. *Voltaire and Beccaria as Reformers of Criminal Law*. New York: Columbia University Press, 1942.

Marks, Alfred. *Tyburn Tree: Its History and Annals*. London: Brown, Langham and Co., 1908.

Masur, Louis P. *Rites of Execution: Capital Punishment and the Transformation of American Culture, 1776–1865*. New York: Oxford University Press, 1989.

Maxcey, Carl E. "Justice and Order: Martin Luther and Thomas More on the Death Penalty and Retribution." *Moreana: Bulletin Thomas More* 20 (1979–80): 17–33.

Mayfield, Noel Henning. *Puritans and Regicide: Presbyterian-Independent Differences over the Trial and Execution of Charles (I) Stuart*. Lanham, Md.: University Press of America, 1988.

Miller, Arthur S., and Jeffrey H. Bowman. *Death by Installments: The Ordeal of Willie Francis*. Westport, Conn.: Greenwood Press, 1988.

Miller, D. A. *The Novel and the Police*. Berkeley and Los Angeles: University of California Press, 1988.

Mingay, G. E., ed. *The Unquiet Countryside*. London: Routledge, 1989.

Murphy, Jeffrie G. *Punishment and Rehabilitation*. Belmont, Calif.: Wadsworth Publishing Company, 1985.

Nakell, Barry, and Kenneth A. Hardy. *The Arbitrariness of the Death Penalty*. Philadelphia: Temple University Press, 1987.

Nathanson, Stephen. *An Eye for an Eye?: The Morality of Punishing by Death*. Totowa, N.J.: Rowman and Littlefield, 1987.

O'Donnell, Bernard. *Should Women Hang?* London: W. H. Allen, 1956.

Oram, Richard W. "George Orwell's 'A Hanging' and Thackeray." *American Notes and Queries* 21 (1983), 108–9.

Otterbein, Keith F. *The Ultimate Coercive Sanction: A Cross-Cultural Study of Capital Punishment.* New Haven, Conn.: HRAF Press, 1986.

Pannick, David. *Judicial Review of the Death Penalty.* London: Duckworth, 1982.

Parry, L. A. *The History of Torture in England.* Montclair, N.J.: Patterson Smith, 1975.

Pearl, Cyril. *Victorian Patchwork.* London: Heinemann, 1972.

Phillipson, Coleman. *Three Criminal Law Reformers: Beccaria, Bentham, Romilly.* London: J. M. Dent, 1923.

Plumb, J. H. *England in the Eighteenth Century, 1714-1815.* New York: Penguin, 1959.

Potter, John Deane. *The Art of Hanging.* South Brunswick, New York: A. S. Barnes, 1969.

Radzinowicz, Leon. *A History of English Criminal Law and Its Administration from 1750.* 5 vols. London: Stevens, 1948-86.

Rolph, C. H. *Common Sense About Crime and Punishment.* London: Gollancz, 1961.

Rutenberg, Daniel. "From Praise of Hanging to the Femme Fatale: Capital Punishment in 'Nineties Periodicals." *Victorian Periodicals Review* 11 (1978): 95-104.

Saleilles, Raymond. *The Individualization of Punishment.* Montclair, N.J.: Patterson Smith, 1968.

Schroeder, Natalie. "Jack Sheppard and Barnaby Rudge: Yet More 'Humbug' from a 'Jolter Head.'" *Studies in the Novel* 18 (Spring 1986): 27-35.

Sellin, Johan Thorsten. *The Penalty of Death.* Newbury Park, Calif: Sage Publications, 1980.

Sheleff, Leon Shaskolsky. *Ultimate Penalties: Capital Punishment, Life Imprisonment, Physical Torture.* Columbus: Ohio State University Press, 1987.

Silberman, Charles E. *Criminal Violence, Criminal Justice.* New York: Random House, 1980.

Simon, Irene. "Stillingfleet's Sermon Preached before the King on the Anniversary of the Execution of Charles I, 30 January 1668/9." In *Studies in Seventeenth-Century English Literature, History, and Bibliography: Festschrift for Professor T. A. Birrell on the Occasion of His Sixtieth Birthday,* edited by G. A. M. Janssens and F. G. A. M. Aarts, 195-210. Amsterdam: Rodopi, 1984.

Sorell, Tom. *Moral Theory and Capital Punishment.* London: Blackwell, 1988.

Streib, Victor L. *Death Penalty for Juveniles.* Bloomington: Indiana University Press, 1987.

Strouse, Evelyn. *The Death Penalty: Issues in the Debate.* New York: Public Affairs Committee, 1987.

Templewood, Samuel John Gurney. *The Shadow of the Gallows*. London: Gollancz, 1951.

Tillotson, Kathleen. "A Letter from Dickens on Capital Punishment." *Times Literary Supplement*, 12 August 1965, 704.

Tobias, J. J. *Crime and Industrial Society in the 19th Century*. New York: Schocken Books, 1967.

Tuttle, Elizabeth Orman. *The Crusade Against Capital Punishment in Great Britain*. London: Stevens; Chicago: Quadrangle Books, 1961.

Van der Elst, Violet. *On the Gallows*. London: Doge Press, 1937.

Warner, Fred B. "The Hanging Judge Once More before the Bar." *Papers of the Bibliographical Society of America* 70 (1976): 89–96. [On R. L. Stevenson.]

White, Welsh S. *The Death Penalty in the Eighties: An Examination of the Modern System of Capital Punishment*. Ann Arbor: University of Michigan Press, 1987.

Williams, Jack K. *Vogues in Villainy: Crime and Punishment in Ante-Bellum South Carolina*. Columbia: University of South Carolina Press, 1959.

Woeller, Waltraud, and Bruce Cassiday. *The Literature of Crime and Detection: An Illustrated History from Antiquity to the Present*. New York: Ungar, 1988.

Zimring, Franklin E., and Gordon Hawkins. *Capital Punishment and the American Agenda*. Cambridge: Cambridge University Press, 1986.

Anthologies, Bibliographies, Collections of Essays, and Encyclopedias

Assassinations and Executions: An Encyclopedia of Political Violence, 1865–1986. Edited by Harris M. Lentz, III. Jefferson, N.C.: McFarland, 1988.

Blood and Knavery: A Collection of English Renaissance Pamphlets and Ballads of Crime and Sin. Edited by Joseph H. Marshburn and Alan R. Velie. Rutherford, N.J.: Farleigh Dickinson University Press, 1973.

Bloody Versicles: The Rhymes of Crime. Edited by Jonathan Goodman. Newton Abbot, Devon, England: David and Charles, 1971. [Poetic justice. Verse and ballads of the 19th and 20th centuries.]

By the Neck: A Book of Hangings. Edited by August Mencken. New York: Hastings House, 1942.

Capital Punishment as a Deterrent: A Bibliography. Compiled by Alan V. Miller. Monticello, Ill.: Vance Bibliographies, 1980.

The Capital Punishment Dilemma, 1950–1977: A Subject Bibliography. Compiled by Charles W. Triche, III. Troy, N.Y.: Whitston Publishing Company, 1979.

Capital Punishment in America: An Annotated Bibliography. Edited by Michael L. Radelet and Margaret Vandiver. New York: Garland, 1988.

Challenging Capital Punishment: Legal and Social Science Approaches. Edited by Kenneth C. Haas and James A. Inciardi. Ithaca, N.Y.: Sage, 1988.

Crime and Punishment. Edited by Kenyon Calthrop. Oxford, England: Pergamon, 1968. [Bibliography. Poetry and prose.]

The Death Penalty: A Literary and Historical Approach. Edited by Edward G. McGehee and William H. Hildebrand. Boston: Heath, 1964.

The Death Penalty and Torture. Edited by Franz Bockle and Jacques Pohier. New York: Seabury Press, 1979.

The Death Penalty in America: An Anthology. Edited by Hugo Adam Bedau. Chicago: Aldine Publishing Company, 1968.

The Death Penalty: Opposing Viewpoints. Edited by Bonnie Szumski, Lynn Hall, and Susan Bursell. St. Paul, Minn.: Greenhaven Press, 1986.

Death Row: Interviews with Inmates, Their Families and Opponents of Capital Punishment. Edited by Shirley Dicks. Jefferson, N.C.: McFarland, 1990.

Essays on the Death Penalty. Edited by Robert Tolbert Ingram. Houston, Tex.: St. Thomas Press, 1963.

Executions, 1601–1926: When, Where, Why, How, Who?: All the Principal Executions for 400 Years. London: Sungolf Plus Leisure Co., 1979.

The Hanging Question: Essays on the Death Penalty. Edited by Louis Jacques Blom-Cooper. London: Duckworth, 1969.

Philosophy of Punishment. Edited by Robert M. Baird and Stuart E. Rosenbaum. Buffalo, N.Y.: Prometheus Books, 1988.

Prison Anthology. Edited by A. G. Stock and Reginald Reynolds. London: Jarrolds, 1938 [Includes section "Dock and scaffold"; Prose and poetry of all periods.]

Problems of Death: Opposing Viewpoints. Edited by David L. Bender. 2d ed. St. Paul, Minn.: Greenhaven Press, 1981.

Reviving the Death Penalty. Compiled by Gary E. McCuen and R. A. Baumgart. Hudson, Wis.: Gary E. McCuen Publications, 1985.

Romanticism and Criminal Justice: A Selection of Papers. Special issue of *Wordsworth Circle* 19, no. 2 (Spring 1988): 65–107.

Voices against Death: American Opposition to Capital Punishment, 1787–1975. Edited by Philip English Mackey. New York: B. Franklin, 1976.

Index

Contributors

John J. Burke, Jr., is professor of English at the University of Alabama, Tuscaloosa. His research interests include Samuel Johnson, Henry Fielding, and theory of fiction. Currently he serves as English/American book review editor for *South Atlantic Review*.

David D. Cooper is the director of the Mercyhurst College Center for Justice and Mental Health Issues in Erie, Pennsylvania. He is a social historian specializing in nineteenth-century British history and has written on crime and punishment of that period. His book *The Lesson of the Scaffold: The Public Execution Controversy in Victorian England* was published jointly in 1974 by the Ohio University Press and Allen Lane.

Barry Faulk is a graduate student in the English department at the University of Illinois at Urbana-Champaign. He has published an essay and a book review on George Moore. He is currently working on a sociological reading of character in early Dickens, primarily *The Pickwick Papers*.

Michael Jasper is a teaching fellow at Kent State University, where he teaches English and Latin. He has published award-winning short fiction in various literary journals in the southeast.

Beth Kalikoff is an associate professor of English at the University of Puget Sound in Tacoma, Washington. She has written on nineteenth-century theater and popular literature as well as on the fallen woman in Victorian literature. Her book *Murder and Moral Decay in Victorian Popular Literature* was published in 1986 by UMI Research Press.

Steven Lynn is an associate professor of English at the University of South Carolina in Columbia, South Carolina. His interests include eighteenth-century literature, the history of rhetoric, and critical theory. He is currently working on a study of Samuel Johnson and deconstruction.

F. S. Schwarzbach is department chairman and professor of English at Washington State University in Pullman, Washington. He is the author of

Dickens and the City (1979) and coeditor of *Victorian Artists and the City: A Collection of Critical Essays* (1980). He is completing a study of Dickens as a social thinker.

Donald T. Siebert is professor of English at the University of South Carolina, Columbia. He has published widely on eighteenth-century subjects, including major figures such as Swift, Pope, Johnson, Lessing, and Hume. His book, *The Moral Animus of David Hume* (1990), won the eighteenth-century manuscript competition sponsored by the University of Delaware Press.

Gayle R. Swanson is associate professor of English at Newberry College in Newberry, South Carolina. She serves as editor of *Studies in Short Fiction* and is coauthor of *Conversations with South Carolina Poets*.

William B. Thesing is professor of English at the University of South Carolina in Columbia. He is the author of *The London Muse: Victorian Poetic Responses to the City* (1982), coauthor of *English Prose and Criticism, 1900–1950* (1983), and editor of two volumes of the *Dictionary of Literary Biography* on *Victorian Prose Writers* (1987). He has also published essays on Hopkins and Arnold. He has taught undergraduate and graduate courses on the topic of crime and the city in nineteenth-century literature.